THE ESSENCE OF
SUCCESS

TWELVE MINI BIOGRAPHIES

FOURTH EDITION

THE ESSENCE OF
SUCCESS
TWELVE MINI BIOGRAPHIES

First Edition published by 20th Century Fax Ltd. in 1998
Second Edition published by HyperOs 2014
Third Edition published by HyperOs 2014
Fourth Edition published by HyperOs 2015

All rights reserved.

CO-EDITORS
Anthony Brito
Mark Crow

WRITERS
Anthony Brito
Mark Crow
Damien Carr
Nicholas Cheek
Terry Savage
Gordon Ritchie

Copyright © HyperDrive Systems Ltd., London 1998-2015

ISBN-13: 978-1503052406
ISBN-10: 1503052400

All Rights Reserved. No part of this publication may be reproduced,
stored in a retrieval system, or transmitted, in any form, or by any
means, electronic, mechanical, photocopying, recording or otherwise,
without the prior permission of the publisher and copyright holder.

CONTENTS

INTRODUCTION

This book is a compilation of twelve concise biographies which will enable the reader to gain an insight into each character in one short sitting.

Rather than reading an exhaustive three hundred page book and becoming an expert on Bill Gates' life, for example, the reader can discover the essential character, motivation and philosophy of the individual in just a few hours. The idea is that during a lunch break or when winding down, you can get an accurate snapshot of someone's entire life.

'A whole life without having to read a whole book.'

This was the concept. But we could not resist investigating a further possibility. We had to ask the question:

'Is there a common factor between these twelve diverse success stories?'

We present a detailed analysis of each of the twelve lives in order to enable the reader to find any common character traits or common experiences shared between them that might have enabled them to succeed so spectacularly. The idea is that the essence of their success can be distilled from these diversity of their paths to it. On completion of the mini-biographies, we realised what the common factor was. We discovered what could be the vital ingredient, the necessary ingredient for outstanding success. This is covered in our conclusion at the end of the book.

The purpose of this book is to provide inspiration to the reader, and to explain that individual views and convictions are as important as the general consensus. No individual mind is inferior to any collection of minds.

An individual can be right if they stand firm in the face of mass opposition. While our study is a contemporary one, we fully realise that the maverick spirit has been evident throughout history. Scientifically men such as Isaac Newton pushed the boundaries of human endeavour. In other eyes, religious figures such as Jesus provide the seminal example of an outsider who epitomised the maverick spirit. It is the realisation that 'the power of one' can make a difference within the world. As long as individuals follow their own unique calling and have the courage to act on their own initiative then the human race as a family, will continue to advance.

RICHARD BRANSON
1950 - PRESENT DAY

When a rebellious Richard Branson left public school at seventeen, his headmaster predicted he would either go to prison or become a millionaire. He never went to prison. Instead, he became probably the most popular and certainly one of the most successful entrepreneurs in Britain. Founder of the billion pound Virgin Group, his interests include airlines, music, soft drinks, pensions, clothing, cosmetics, cinemas and railways. When discussion began for a new Mayor of London in 1997, Branson topped all popularity polls, without even declaring an interest. He is a business maverick whose dare-devil ballooning exploits have captured the media's attention and the public's imagination.

Richard Charles Nicholas Branson was born on the 18 July 1950. His father was a barrister. His mother, Eve Branson, owned an embroidery business, a former air hostess and gliding instructor, decided her son would also become a high-flyer. Richard, she resolved, would become Prime Minister. The Bransons were a colourful family. Eve's sister, Clare, was known for her love of parachuting, and was the epitome of independence as she swanned around smoking her favourite cigars. Richard was also inspired by tales of a distant relative, the famous Antarctic explorer, Captain Scott.

Eve impressed on her son the idea that shyness was a weakness which would not be tolerated in her home. A prime example of how she sought to instil independence in Richard, took place when he was only four years old. She reputedly stopped her car about half a mile from their intended destination and told him to try to make it back to his grandfather's farmhouse alone. Richard obliged and took his first steps into the unknown. By nightfall there was still no sign of the intrepid toddler. Eventually a phone call came from a neighbouring farm; Richard had wandered off in the wrong direction, and had ended up a mile away.

At seven, Branson was challenged to swim across a river for the reward of £1. The family watched as the child plucked up the courage and dived in. He struggled against the current but finally made it to the other side, where he proudly collected his winnings. Courage and confidence were the cornerstones of his family education. However, the attitude to challenge everything that stood in his way caused problems. He did not take well to authority or rules, and at school was seen as undisciplined and wilful.

Branson's first steps into the business world were ambitious (if somewhat ludicrous). Unfortunately, teenage money-making schemes to grow Christmas trees and breed budgerigars did not have quite the commercial impact the young entrepreneur had hoped.

He fell behind in his school work and, faced with the common entrance examnecessary for public school, was sent for a year's intensive tuition at a prep school. Responding to the encouragement of his parents, he passed. In September 1964, he was accepted at Stowe School in Buckinghamshire. From the outset, Branson stood out at Stowe, and not for all the right reasons. He lacked interest in both the academic and cultural aspects of the school. Teachers noted his wandering mind and fickle attitude. According to his former tutor, Brian Stephan: 'It was apparent that his one aim was to get on and out into the world. His fellow pupils perceived him as a sort of loose cannon.'

Yet, on occasions he would show signs of prodigious potential. His scepticism towards the institution was not passive. In fact, his first major business venture came as the result of his opposition to school protocol. He had sent a letter to the headmaster protesting against certain regulations. His suggestions were rejected. Incensed, Branson and a friend, Jonathan Holland-Gems, thought of a way to vent their frustration. The teenagers came up with the idea of Student, a magazine to cater for their own age-group.

He later reflected, 'I never intended to become an entrepreneur. I was 15, didn't like the way I was being taught, wanted to get out of school and put the world right, so I started the magazine.'

Branson employed his charisma to cajole fellow pupils into helping out with rough drafts of the magazine. He forgot about his academic work and devoted all his energy to his big idea. In his final year of O-Levels he expressed reservations about continuing his education. This caused concern to family and teachers, who felt that he should at least complete his A-Levels before leaving Stowe. In 1967, he made a firm decision to abandon his studies, and managed to sell the idea to his parents. At last he was free to pursue his own agenda.

Free from the constraints of public school, Branson moved to London with Holland-Gems to work on Student. They set up in the basement of the Holland-Gems family home. With limited finance and unlimited enthusiasm, they gathered a small band of casual employees to get the project off the ground. The first issue was released in 1968. Branson had worked intensively to promote the magazine. He had written to world leaders, poets, actors and singers for their views. He even received a reply from the President of the United States, Lyndon Johnson, expressing support. The dynamic young editor had engineered a wave of publicity, and was soon touted as a bright prospect throughout the press.

Branson was a natural businessman. He wanted the venture to be fun but was very serious about making it a success. A measure of just how seriously he took his new career was illustrated when the nineteen year old issued a high court writ against Beatles singer, John Lennon. Branson had made an agreement with Lennon's agent for a new recording to be included with a copy of the magazine. When the song failed to materialise, Branson displayed the boldness to stand up to the millionaire celebrity. The matter never went to court, but the young entrepreneur had made his point.

During the same period Branson opened the Student Advisory Centre, an organisation to deal with health issues. This was borne out of his own personal experience: when a girlfriend had become unintentionally pregnant they had found the process of learning about and arranging an abortion extremely difficult and traumatic. He decided to provide young people with the information and advice from which he could have once benefited.

Late in 1969, Student (rather aptly) found itself in financial difficulty. Branson decided to close the magazine and focus on a new idea. He believed he could undercut high-street record stores by selling cheap imports by post. Virgin mail order was an immediate success. In future years he would cultivate the Virgin brand name to an unprecedented level of success. The distinctive red and white logo would become synonymous with both youthful energy and reliability.

A year later, Branson gave his business partner and childhood friend, Nick Powell, a 40 percent share in Virgin. The ability to bring the right people on board would be crucial to the growth of the his empire. Branson's former girlfriend, Mandy Ellis, explains how the two friends made a formidable partnership; Virgin consisted of 'Richard going out and splattering the world with ideas, and Nick coming along behind them, tidying up, budgeting them and holding them together.' The picture is of a creative, if rather erratic figure; but one who is aware of his limitations and able to collaborate with more down-to-earth, steady associates.

In 1971, Branson began a whirlwind affair with the woman who was to become the first Mrs Branson - a beautiful nineteen year old American named Kirsten Tomassi. In typically freewheeling style, Branson 'snatched' her from her musician boyfriend (who was working at Branson's music studio The Manor) and housed her on his houseboat. By the summer of 1972 they were married.

Branson almost fulfilled both parts of his headmaster's prediction when during a business trip to Europe he discovered a convenient way to avoid customs tax. Customs officials caught on to the fraud, and Branson was arrested. He faced going to jail, but managed to persuade the tax officials to let him pay back all the tax instead. He faced a bill of over £50,000, but crucially avoided a criminal record and was allowed to keep his business.

In 1971, his mail order business was threatened by a Post Office strike. Faced with a dangerous loss of sales, Branson decided to expand by establishing a record shop in Oxford Street. By 1972, there were fourteen Virgin record stores around the country. It was becoming one of the largest chain stores in Britain. Branson later accounted for the success by pointing to the atmosphere in the shops, which was more akin to a Beatnik club than a business. The following year he set up a recording studio for his own record label. Virgin Records released its first album in 1973; it comprised three tracks from an artist who had been turned down by every major record label over the past few years. The artist was Mike Oldfield and his album Tubular Bells became one of the all time best sellers.

The continued success of the label can be attributed to a shrewd act of delegation by Branson. He left the signing of the artists to Simon Draper, a person who was seen as something of a cultural barometer. Draper signed the irascible Sex Pistols 1977, and the chart-topping Culture Club in the early 80's. Other notable signings included Simple Minds, Phil Collins and The Human League.

However, while his business flourished, his three year marriage to Kirsten was in trouble. Sexual incompatibility led to a night of experimental wife swapping for the couple which resulted in Kirsten meeting her new partner and walking out on Branson. After a similar beginning to their relationship, the finale could be seen as somewhat ironic.

By 1978, Branson could afford his own piece of Caribbean paradise, buying Neckar Island for $300,000. Two years later, he branched out into a new venture and bought a night-club, Heaven, under the arches in Charing Cross. The clientele was predominantly gay, the club controversial, the acquisition risky. Yet, it was to prove another good decision: Heaven remains one of London's most popular venues while other clubs have struggled or fallen by the wayside. However, if Branson's Midas touch seemed inexorable, on one front he was failing. In 1981, he had to admit defeat and close another magazine. Event, which was supposed to rival the entertainment magazine Time Out, became a non-event, losing Branson over £750,000.

Meanwhile, in his personal life, Branson had failed to win Kirsten back. By 1976, he had admitted defeat and sought out the next Mrs Branson - Joan Templeman. The simple fact that she was married did not hinder Branson, it just made it more of a challenge. A few months after the start of the affair, Joan's marriage was over. In 1981, their first child, Holly, was born; four years later she had a brother, Sam. It was to be a further five years before the couple were married. Once more, Branson had refused to let convention dictate.

In 1985, Branson was approached by the American businessman, Randolph Fields, who impressed upon him the idea of starting up a small airline franchise. Branson viewed the idea as an exciting challenge, and he was not in the habit of turning down a challenge. With Fields as chairman, the Virgin Atlantic project began in earnest. Over the next few years, Fields began to sense that he was being marginalised. The tension grew until he believed he had no option but to take the company to court. He argued that Virgin were systematically omitting him from key decisions, the judge agreed. Fields took a pay off and took his leave. Branson took total control of the airline.

In his quest to gain publicity for his airline, Branson needed an excuse to hog the media limelight. The perfect opportunity arose when he met up with a team seeking sponsorship for an Atlantic crossing by speedboat. Branson hijacked the venture, and it was his face that was splashed all over the newspapers. The Virgin Atlantic Challenger attempted its crossing on 12 August 1985. But with a hundred miles to go before they reached Britain, the boat was holed by floating debris. Branson and the crew were forced into lifeboats, to watch their record-breaking hopes sink beneath the waves. Yet, the crossing had caught the media's attention, who were by now fascinated by the adventurous businessman. A year later, a second Challenger attempt was a success. Branson and the crew won the coveted 'Blue Ribbon' for the fastest transatlantic sea crossing.

If Branson's friends and associates had been impressed by his Challenger crossing, his next adventure would exceed all expectations. Two years after the speedboat attempt, an Atlantic crossing was again on the agenda - but this time by balloon. With the expertise of Per Lindstrand as pilot, the two set out on their adventure. Nearing Ireland, their intended destination, they realised there was too much fuel on board for a safe landing. To make matters worse, they lost all electrical power and were forced to make a landing at sea. As Lindstrand dived into the sea, co-pilot Branson remained stranded in the capsule as a gust of wind took it thousands of feet above the water, lie sat helpless, scribbling a last note to his family, only for the balloon to descend gently back into the sea. Both survived the harrowing experience. Rather than calming Branson's adventurous spirit, the episode further fuelled his ballooning ambitions. In 1991, the duo would fly again, this time covering a record-breaking 6,700 miles across the Pacific Ocean. Six years later, they would unsuccessfully attempt to circumnavigate the globe.

Back in 1986, Branson moved, in tabloid speak, 'from the rock market to the stock market.' During the proposed move to float Virgin as a public company, Branson gave his colleagues another taste of his adventurous spirit. On one of his parachute jumps, he came perilously close to death. Instead of pulling the rip-cord to release the parachute, he somehow managed to release the entire pack from his back. He fell thousands of feet but was miraculously saved by his instructors. As usual the incident did not curb his passion for adrenaline, but it certainly gave his financial advisors a scare.

In October 1987, stock markets around the world crashed. Branson knew the danger, if his brand-name became associated with the public's financial loss, it would take years to rebuild the Virgin name. Thus, he implemented a management buyout in 1988 in which no investor lost any money. He was very aware that he had to retain a reputation for scrupulous honesty. He also outlined the belief that 'being an entrepreneur and the chairman of a public company just doesn't mix.' Just as when he had left public school, he needed the freedom and the undiluted power to follow his instincts.

The Virgin tycoon pursues his business interests with the same risk-taking bravado that drives his 'leisure' pursuits. In 1988, his airline made a modest profit in the face of strong competition from its much larger rivals. Instead of seeking to consolidate his position, he gambled by expanding into the Japanese market. His business advisors and the Virgin board were apprehensive about the huge financial risk involved in setting up routes to Tokyo. But by 1990, Branson's stubborn vision was vindicated - the airline's turnover had doubled to £180m.

A year later, he found himself at the centre of a vindictive smear campaign by his arch business rival, British Airways. BA hired private detectives, published scurrilous stories in the national press and used PR champion Frank Basham to 'dish the dirt'. If BA didn't know quite what they were up against, Basham certainly did, once remarking: 'Branson displays what can only be characterised as a Houdini like ability to escape from tight corners.' Branson compiled a catalogue of complaints against BA, whom he believed were aggressively poaching his customers and trying to discredit him. He uncovered evidence of an organised conspiracy by senior BA management to force him and his company out of the airline industry. He took BA to court, winning compensation of £500,000 and an apology. A brilliant piece of Branson PR, he divided his award equally among his staff.

Alongside the success and brilliant self promotion, there were, inevitably, setbacks. One of his greatest disappointments occurred in 1994 when the UK Lottery Foundation, a consortium under his leadership, failed to win the contract for Britain's new National Lottery. He had pledged that all profits would go to good causes and was incensed when the Government awarded the franchise to Camelot, a profit-making consortium. The pain was compounded by the fact that he had originally suggested the idea of a national lottery to the government six years earlier. For once it was his idea that had been hijacked. He told listeners of BBC Radio Four: 'It is completely and utterly wrong for the government to award the Lottery and profits to a handful of companies when they are not taking any risks.. .Of all the decisions I have ever seen any government make over many, many years I reckon this is perhaps the most crass.'

But Branson had the last laugh. Early in 1998, he convinced a high court jury that Guy Snowden, the chief executive of GTECH and part owner of Camelot, had attempted to bribe him out of bidding for the lottery license. Branson won the case and received £100,000 in damages. This time the money went to charity.

In 1996, Branson embarked on another high risk venture, when he bought into the West Coast train service formally controlled by British Rail. His aim was to make the dilapidated service as comfortable and as efficient as his airline. Critics felt that his impulsive acquisition, along with certain others, could be a step too far for the Virgin Group. Guardian writer Mark Lawson, quipped: '[Branson] has rapidly expanded from airlines to fizzy drinks to financial investments to cinemas to clothes and now railways, many have felt that level of promiscuity should be recognised by formally changing the company's trade name from Virgin to Whore.'

Critics of Branson's strategy do have some justification. The Virgin rail service remains something of a national joke and his clothing and cosmetics firm, Victory Corporation, recorded a loss of £19m in August 1998. Yet, it is still early days for both ventures, and elsewhere the Virgin empire continues to flourish. Branson remains as popular and as visible as ever; it would surely be naive to write him off.

In September 1998, Branson's long-awaited autobiography, Losing my Virginity, was launched amid clamorous publicity. Accounts of wife-swapping and drug-taking were splashed across the British press. At the centre of it all was the bearded self-publicist, who even posed naked (apart from his strategically placed book) for the occasion. Another ballooning expedition to circumnavigate the world beckons for Branson. At the age of forty nine, the adventurous spirit instilled so early in life, remains undiminished. In his autobiography he sums up the attitude which has taken him to the top - 'my interests in life come from setting myself huge and unachievable challenges and then rising above them.'

BILL GATES
1955 - PRESENT DAY

In 1995, Bill Gates was named by Forbes as the world's richest individual, with a personal wealth of $20 billion. Several years later, some estimates broke the $50 billion mark. Gates' transformation from computer-obsessed adolescent to billionaire businessman is one of the most compelling success stories of our age. In the ruthless world of the computer industry, riven with bitter rivalries and personal feuds, Gates was able to steer his software company Microsoft - right to the top. In 1988, Microsoft overtook General Electric to become the world's biggest company, valued at $261 billion. To many Gates is the ultimate entrepreneur, to others a monopolist intent on destroying all competition by any means necessary.

William H. Gates III was born to a well-to-do Seattle couple on 28 October 1955. From his parents, an attorney and a schoolteacher, he gained an inquisitive mind and a passion for education. The young Gates, encouraged by his ambitious parents, developed a thirst for knowledge that has never abated. At eight, he became obsessed with encyclopedias. Aged eleven, he revelled in the role of class clown at his first school. His parents, alarmed at their son's underachievement and disruptive behaviour, sent him to a psychiatrist. Gates, inspired by the expert, was soon more interested in expanding his mind than entertaining his classmates.

An infatuation with computers began when he moved to the private Lakeside School. The unlikely source of a Mothers' Club 'Jumble Sale' provided the expensive rarity of an early computer. It was slow, cumbersome and screenless; the thirteen year-old schoolboy was immediately hooked. Along with his inseparable friend Paul Allen, the boys began their precocious programming careers. If their first software program for playing tic-tac-toe was harmless fun, the commercial viability of their new hobby was soon apparent. The teenagers earned in excess of $4000 for writing an academic scheduling program for the school. A few tweaks to the program and Gates found himself in classes full of girls; but, sadly, to no avail - he was already branded a computer nerd.

The desire for control and power was clearly behind his early affection for computing. He could give orders and make demands of the computer; fellow humans were less easy to influence. He outlines this attraction in his book, The Road Ahead: 'I realized later that part of the appeal must have been that here was an enormous, expensive, grown-up machine and we, the kids, could control it. We were too young to drive or do any of the things adults could have fun at, but we could give this big machine orders and it would always obey.'

Gates was a determined scholar, but all his major achievements were the product of individual drive and initiative. 'I enjoyed school', he later commented, 'but I pursued my strongest interests independently.' This chimes with his long-held belief that education is the responsibility of the individual not the institution. An enterprising self-starter from the beginning, Gates used his school holidays and free time making deals with computer companies, exchanging his ability to write software for access to the latest technology.

In 1972, the friends were ecstatic when they read about a new microprocessor chip made by Intel. They used this innovation to construct the 'Traf-O-Data' - a machine to measure and analyse traffic flow. Not for the last time the boys were disappointed when their contraption bombed at a demonstration, and no one wanted to buy it. But Gates and Allen were quick to spot the potential of the microprocessor, and their interest would pay dividends.

Gates entered Harvard University in 1973. Sensitive to his reputation as a nerd, he postured as a poker-playing 'slacker'. He would make a point of skipping classes and playing all-night poker games, only to cram feverishly at the end of term to achieve the perfect grades. He was also known to frequent a seedy area of Boston, known as the Combat Zone - home to hookers and adult entertainment. He switched from economics to mathematics, unsure of his academic bearings. In 1975, he dropped out altogether. It was the best decision of an undistinguished academic career. 1975 was also the year he co-founded Microsoft.

At Harvard, Gates had kept in close contact with Paul Allen. One day Allen rushed his friend to a newsstand in Harvard Square to show him the latest issue of Popular Electronics. As they read about the launch of the first personal computer, the Altair 8800, they were infused with a sense of destiny. Gates was convinced 'it would change us and the world of computing.' He was right. The feeling of excitement was compounded by a fear that they might have 'missed the boat'. But the PC revolution was still in its infancy and its future was up for grabs. Desperate for a piece of the action, Allen quit his job and Gates ditched his degree. They set up Microsoft and ploughed all their energy and resources into the development of software. Allen also had eyes for the computer hardware market, but Gates' instinct to focus on software was inspired. The two-man shoe-string operation would grow into one of the most powerful and profitable companies in the world.

Yet success seldom comes easy. The friends had previously written to all the big computer companies offering to write a computer language for the first Intel chip. They had no takers. Now they frantically sought to do the same for the new Altair computer. Things were not made easier by the fact that they did not even have access to the Altair. They succeeded, but Gates later recalled the strain of the endeavour: 'I did a lot of rocking and pacing in my dorm room the winter of 1975. Paul and I didn't sleep much and lost track of night and day. When I did fall asleep, it was usually at my desk or on the floor. Some days I didn't eat or see anyone.'

Bill Gates was undeniably a real enthusiast and a talented programmer, but he was also much more. From the beginning he was a businessman, comfortable negotiating deals with senior executives, and constantly updating the strategies that would give his company the edge. It is one thing to design a product, quite another to sell it. In the early years of the company, while colleagues focused solely on the technical side. Gates personally undertook the financial, sales and marketing responsibilities. He was still in his teens. Furthermore, his considerable ability to capitalize on promising ideas, not necessarily his own, and flair at the short-term strategic alliances so prevalent in the computer industry, would prove invaluable.

The first alliance was with the makers of the Altair, MITS. Gates and Allen moved the company to Albuquerque, New Mexico, to be close to their client. However, a row with their patron over the ownership of the newly developed software ended the agreement. When MITS were taken over by another company and ceased payment, Microsoft struggled for a year without income, pending a lengthy legal case. Microsoft won the case but were shaken by the ordeal. Gates initiated a rule that in future his company would always have enough cash to function for at least a year without payment. He subsequently described his 'whole experience with the computer industry' as 'a series of economic lessons.' He had learned his first lesson, but had not fought his last legal battle.

In 1980, Gates received a visit from two representatives of IBM the undisputed market leader. They wanted help with the software for a new personal computer - the standard setting IBM PC. Gates originally directed them to his friend Gary Kildall, the founder of Digital Research, but he was away on business. When they returned. Gates undertook the project himself. After purchasing ideas and personnel from a tiny company - Seattle Computer - the Microsoft Disk Operating System (MS-DOS) was born. This would prove the making of Microsoft. Before he died, Kildall published his memoirs, alleging that the Microsoft system was a clone of his original work. Of Gates he was especially scathing: 'I have grown up in this industry with Gates. I le is divisive. He is manipulative. He is a user.'

The IBM PC originally shipped with the choice of three operating systems. Gates offered the Microsoft version at a knockdown price to vastly undercut the rival systems - 'we practically gave the software to IBM.' he later conceded. His plan was to make his profit by licensing DOS to other computer companies seeking to emulate IBM's success. His strategy could not have worked better. The more expensive rival systems were ditched, the IBM PC became the standard, and Microsoft duly became the software standard. All the companies seeking IBM compatibility licensed MS-DOS, and the Bill Gates stranglehold over the software market had begun.

The idea of a graphical user interface was nothing new when Microsoft announced plans to bring it to the IBM PC in 1983. The notion that the user could click on images using a 'mouse' rather than having to type in obscure commands, became an essential factor in die 'PC revolution'. Gates christened his graphical system 'Windows'. Much of the Windows technology relied heavily on the innovative work of the Xerox Palo Alto Research Center. Yet, typically, it would take the Microsoft front-man to really cash-in on these innovations.

Microsoft continued their collaboration with IBM on another operating system (OS/2). However, this was to prove an acrimonious project, plagued by disagreements, and culminating in Microsoft leaving the venture. Gates termed the incident 'the scariest threat to Microsoft's future ever,' he explained 'We had to compete against the largest company in the computer industry, which was fighting us with the operating system software we had helped develop.' Yet, if Gates was seriously worried, he need not have concerned himself. OS/2 failed and the IBM star was on the wane. The rift left Microsoft with the time to concentrate fully on Windows. In concert with subsequent applications such as Word (word-processor), Excel (spreadsheet) and Access (database), Windows would come to be the conclusive step in Microsoft's domination. Gates later boasted to Playboy: 'We bet the company on Windows and we deserve to benefit. It was a risk that paid off immensely.' With every new version of Windows, Gates tightened his stranglehold. Windows 95 shipped an astonishing 20 million copies in the year of its release. Soon more than ninety percent of personal computers relied on Microsoft operating systems.

On its tenth anniversary (1985) Microsoft could boast annual sales figures of $140 million. Five years later its revenues exceeded the $1 billion mark. In 1994, it could afford to spend $100 million on a global advertising campaign to share their enthusiasm for computers with the world. As part of the much hyped, and much delayed, launch of Windows 95, it has been suggested that as much as $12 million was paid for use of the Rolling Stones song, 'Start Me Up'. The sprawling Microsoft corporate campus at Redmond played host to the glitzy launch party, where comedian Jay Leno was a surprise guest. International marketing strategies went into overdrive before the 12:00 AM product launch. Computer stores around the world remained open, eagerly anticipating the midnight consumer feeding frenzy.

By this stage, criticism of the youngest American billionaire and his excessively profitable company was rife. Microsoft was accused of being over-aggressive and monopolistic. Gates was branded an egomaniac, prepared to go to extreme lengths to dispose of his opponents. Many of his business battles ended in court. In 1994 Microsoft was forced to pay $120 million in damages to Stac Electronics for patent infringement. Microsoft and its powerful chairman had made numerous enemies. Phillipe Kahn, founder of Borland International, believed Gates was obsessed with destroying his database business. Workers at Microsoft went as far as to have 'Delete Phillipe' T-shirts printed, one even finding its way to the Borland boss. At the time Kahn made no secret of his own personal hostility: 'Gates looks at everything as something that should be his. He acts in any way he can to make it his(There is not an ounce of conscientiousness or compassion in him. The notion of fairness means nothing to him.'

Microsoft first came under federal scrutiny in 1990 due to its 'collusion' with IBM. When the companies fell out soon after, the reason for an investigation was removed, but accusations of unfair practice persisted. There was no shortage of companies prepared to brief the Federal Trade Commission on Microsoft's shortcomings. Microsoft's licensing arrangement with PC manufacturers was one area under scrutiny. The software giant had long offered a sizable discount on DOS if a royalty was paid for every computer shipped. Because the manufacturers were paying for Microsoft DOS with every computer anyway, there was no incentive for them to offer an alternative operating system. Further, there was much talk of 'traps' in Microsoft operating systems which ensured rival applications would have problems. Additionally, Microsoft was accused of utilizing 'vaporware' a fairly common practice in the industry, where the release of a software product is announced a long time before it is ready. This tactic can drastically reduce the demand for a new rival product, as the market naively awaits the release of the unfinished software (or 'vaporware').

In 1997, Gates was incensed to hear that a three-year FTC investigation of his company had been taken over by the US Department of Justice. The investigation centred on allegations that Microsoft was using its near monopoly of operating systems and considerable influence over PC manufacturers to promote its own Internet browser, Explorer, at the expense of a rival browser, Netscape's Navigator. Netscape were the much-lauded newcomers of the industry; some even said they were the next Microsoft. While Gates was occupied with other things, the small and more innovative company set its sights on the Internet. In May 1995 Gates had sent out a desperate memo entitled 'Internet Tidal Wave' stressing the vital importance of die Net to his company's future. But Netscape had opened up a clear lead, and the Microsoft chairman was far from happy. His frustrated attempts to buy Netscape, followed by the attempt to muscle the newcomer out of its lead, seemed to vindicate the views of some of Bill Gates' fiercest critics. Unlike its new rival, Microsoft could afford to simply throw its browser in for free with its Windows software. Gates was once again trying to price his competitors out of the market. But this time Microsoft's well publicized corporate might just made it look like a bully. The damage to its well manicured image was considerable.

Gates was distinctly aggrieved by the adverse publicity. He argued that there was nothing inevitable about his success or its continuation, and that to penalize his prosperity was unfair. In his book The Road Ahead he asserted 'Microsoft is not unstoppable. We have to earn our leadership position every day. If we stop innovating or stop adjusting our plans, or if we miss the next big turn in the industry's road, we'll lose out.' Perhaps Gates' obsession with staying ahead of the market helps to explain, if not excuse, some of his company's more predatory practices.

Microsoft is largely centred around the cult-status of a chairman, whose enthusiasm and ruthlessness shapes its culture. New recruits, mostly young graduates, are expected to devote all energies to the cause, working exhaustive hours in order to come up with the goods. Rather than sitting back on his achievements Gates insists on a hands on approach. He loves to tour the Redmond campus and hear the latest ideas, praising some employees, while humiliating others with his trademark put-down, 'That's about the stupidest thing I've ever heard! ' As he relished the poker games at Harvard, so he thrives in the strategic battles in the computer industry. He clearly revels in his wealth and the lifestyle it affords, craving the thrill of driving his Porsche or Ferrari late at night. In 1994, he paid over $30 million for a Leonardo da Vinci manuscript.

The demonic image of Gates often portrayed in the media, sometimes appears ill at ease with the childish and unkempt individual, whose mother reportedly still chose his clothes well into middle age. In The Road Ahead he sought to highlight his optimism, stressing the positive power of technology to improve education, stimulate communication and increase democracy. In response to the techno-doubters. He pointed to the initial scepticism aroused by historic innovations such as the printing-press and rail-road. On a less revolutionary note, he touted the wallet PC, a pocket sized mini-computer, as the next big thing. For those seeking signs of nerdish eccentricity, plans for a $50 million interactive house made compulsive reading. Guests would be fitted with an electronic pin so the house could identify them, and personalize their progress through its subterranean rooms with music and imagery from its archive. Each room would bloom into life moments before they entered and recede into darkness as soon as they left.

It came as a shock to many when news spread that the notorious bachelor was to marry. The lavish event occurred on New Year's Day, 1994, on the beautiful Hawaiian island of Lanai. That the island was privately owned helped to keep out the prying eye of the media, although the usual battle of wits between security and press reporters made for some entertaining articles. The marriage to smart Microsoft manager Melinda French would inevitably prove a watershed in the tycoon's life. Stories of wild bachelor parties with girls hired to swim naked in his pool, were consigned to history. Married life certainly resulted in a more presentable Bill Gates; the scruffy unwashed image became another relic of the past. No one was happier for Bill than his mother. Mary Gates managed to attend the open-air ceremony despite suffering from terminal cancer. Soon after she was taken into hospital, and passed away in her sleep the same year. Mother and son had been extremely close. As a teacher, long-time regent of the University of Washington, and director of numerous boards, she had been an inspiration. No doubt, his wife and new daughter (born April 1996) helped Gates to come to terms with the loss.

However, rivals who banked on the family man losing his competitive edge were always going to be disappointed. Gates had his eye firmly on the Internet, and the upstarts at Netscape. The world's richest company led by the world's wealthiest man was never likely to surrender its position. Determined not to miss out on new markets or be left behind, he invested his immense resources into numerous ventures. In 1995, Microsoft teamed up with Dreamworks SKG, the film company partly owned by Steven Spielberg, in order to pursue the burgeoning multimedia entertainment market. Through such investments, and many more, Gates hopes to ensure survival amid the hi-tech markets of the future.

Without question the drive, optimism and ruthlessness of Bill Gates underpins his immense success. Hard-headed business sense and technical skill proved a powerful combination. But Gates must also be viewed as the product of the numerous personal and legal battles he has survived. The high-profile and merciless leadership that made Microsoft so effective, also left him an obvious target for criticism. As Microsoft faces a landmark anti-trust case against the federal government, dubbed 'Goliath versus Goliath', key questions must be faced. Would the US government really cripple one of its most successful assets? How would Microsoft cope if its alleged monopoly was broken? Whatever the answers, it's a safe bet that a certain poker enthusiast still has a number of cards to play.

NELSON MANDELA
1918 - 2013

Prisoner 466/64 spent the best part of three decades behind bars. Unlike other long-term inmates, his crime was to relentlessly oppose a regime that actively promoted racial oppression. In 1994, only four years after his release, the prisoner became President of South Africa. This is no ordinary story because Nelson Mandela is no ordinary individual. Our century's most famous political prisoner has become one of its most admired politico I leaders.

Nelson Mandela was born on July 18, 1918. His tribal birth-name, Rolihlandla, translates as 'troublemaker' in the Xhosa language. (It would be seven years before he was given his western name.) His father, Gadla Henry, reigned as village chief. His mother, Nosekeni, was the third of Gadla's four wives. Born into a privileged family, Mandela was informed that his great-grandfather was once king of the Thembu people. Nevertheless, even with this royal background, he spent his early years like every other child in the village, herding the sheep and cattle on the rural plains.

At this time, the European colonial powers had consolidated their rule over the tribes of southern Africa and were systematically imposing tighter restrictions on their land rights and their place in the wider society. Mandela, along with other African children of his generation, revelled in the heroic stories of the ancestral chiefs and warriors who ruled the land before the coming of the European. He would also marvel at accounts of past tribal leaders who fought bravely against the British and Dutch armies to protect their homeland.

Against this political backdrop, his father decided that only education could allow Mandela to progress within such a Euro-centric environment. At seven, he began his education. As was the custom in British mission schools, his teacher gave him his European name. He would come to realise that his new name was as much a denial of African culture as it was a celebration of British history. Nevertheless, Mandela was given a British education as a ticket into the colonial world.

Two years later, his father died. At such an early age, Mandela had to face up to the first turning point of his life. It would have certainly spelled the end of his education, were it not for his family's royal connections. He was taken in by the Thembu regent, Chief Dalindyebo, to be groomed for a position within the royal court. A stern disciplinarian in life, Gadla's influence on his young son would not end with his death. His legacy was one of discipline, honour and dignity - an education that was, in its own way, equal to anything the missionary school had to offer.

Mandela's new home was a total contrast to the rural village where he was raised. But his guardian did share Gadla's enthusiasm for education, and so placed Mandela, along with his own son, into one of the best schools available to black Africans. He progressed through high school and was accepted to study at Fort Hare University. Mandela became active within the university, joining a number of groups, including the student union. He became embroiled in a strike against the university authorities, which escalated to the point where the students involved were threatened with expulsion. All backed down except for a small band spearheaded by Mandela. Out of principle he decided to leave the university rather than acquiesce, much to the annoyance of his guardian. This stubborn refusal to bow under pressure, regardless of the consequences, was one of the character traits that would win the hearts of his people, while enraging his enemies.

However, to many at the royal court, Mandela's actions were disrespectful rather than impressive. To make matters worse, the young man further incurred the wrath of his guardian by defying his attempts to arrange a marriage for him. Mandela would dictate his own future. Favouring adventure over security - he fled. He explains: 'At 23, my guardian felt that it was time for me to get married...But he was no democrat and did not think it worthwhile to consult me about a wife. He selected a girl, fat and dignified, paid a lobola (bride price of) 108 (rand) and arrangements were afoot for the wedding. I escaped to Johannesburg.'

In a hostile environment with little money, Mandela began to build a new life. At this time, Johannesburg was a segregated city. Labourers from all races flocked there in search of riches from the famed gold mines. The city was a hard and unforgiving place, for black Africans it was invariably difficult, each needing a work permit to find even the most menial employment. Mandela eventually found a position as a night watchman. He took naturally to roles of responsibility, an air of authority characterising every undertaking. He was slowly consigning the rural royal court to his past, intent on making it in the big city.

The brash young man, always confident in his abilities, was taken on as a clerk. It was unusual for law firms to employ Africans, but Mandela was fortunate in finding a liberal employer. At the company he gained invaluable legal experience. However, political aspirations were always to the front of his thinking, and, in 1944, he joined the African National Congress. In the same year, he founded the ANC Youth League with Walter Sisulu and Oliver Tambo - two friends who would become life-long political allies. Mandela also married a young nurse, Evelyn Mase.

After a few years, Mandela and Tambo decided to unite their personal and political ambitions, by planning to open a law firm to assist the black population. But first, Mandela had to qualify as a solicitor. It would take all the finances he and his new wife could muster to pay for his studies. Once qualified, he made an almost immediate impact in the courtroom. It was unusual to see a black man addressing the court or cross-examining witnesses (especially if they were in positions of power). But as Mandela struggled for a more open and just society, the white electorate had other ideas. In 1948, the Afrikaner Nationalist party was voted into power - their first act was to enforce the apartheid regime.

Mandela continued to climb the ANC hierarchy. His enthusiasm and commitment - which he had demonstrated by organising youth rallies and meetings - was formally recognised when he was elected President of the Transvaal branch in 1952. In the same year, he was elected Deputy National President of the ANC. With his new responsibility, he pushed for mobilisation on a national scale, in protest against the repressive laws imposed by the Afrikaner regime. His closest ally, Oliver Tambo, explained their objections: 'South African apartheid laws turn innumerable innocent people into criminals. Apartheid stirs hatred and frustration among people. Young people who should be in school or learning a trade, roam the streets, join gangs and wreak their revenge on the society that confronts them with only the dead-end alley of crime or poverty.'

In his first major clash with the government, Mandela found himself under substantial pressure. In 1953, he was ordered by the authorities to resign his position within the ANC; he also received a nine month suspended prison sentence for his role in a mass protest which called for the 'Defiance of Unjust Laws'. Undeterred by the restrictions, Mandela and his fellow activists continued to devise plans to disrupt the government. Unfortunately, they had seriously underestimated the lengths to which their enemy would go to subdue their protest.

Mandela refined his political philosophy as he became more deeply entrenched in the ANC's fight against apartheid. In his early twenties, he had solely advocated pro-African views. This outlook changed as he realised that politics based solely on racial difference would be just as negative as white domination in South Africa. He still regarded himself as an African nationalist, but now his vision was of a harmonious multi-cultural nation. This, of course, was an aim which was acutely difficult to discredit.

During the 1950s, the ANC helped to compile a report that outlined their grievances and made specific demands of the government. The 'Freedom Charter' was widely hailed a success. Unfortunately, their hopes were shattered, as the government arrested over 150 antiapartheid activists, including Mandela, and charged them with treason. If found guilty, they faced the death penalty. The trial began in 1956, with the defendants confident of the government's lack of evidence. Yet, if there was a sense of complacency from the accused, then, this soon evaporated when Oswald Pirow was named Chief Prosecutor. He was known for his right-wing views, and a dislike for blacks, Jews and communists. He had even stated publicly that Hitler 'was the greatest man of his age.'

By this time, Mandela's personal life was fast disintegrating. His political crusade was seriously hindering his relationship with his wife and family. Evelyn had reached a point where she could see no point in staying in the marriage. Feeling overlooked and powerless to make Mandela resemble anything close to a husband and father, she left the family home with their three children. They divorced in the same year. In his 1994 autobiography, Mandela confessed: 'For myself, I have never regretted my commitment to the struggle, and I was always prepared to face the hardships that affected me personally. But my family paid a terrible price, perhaps too dear a price, for my commitment. I did not in the beginning choose to place my people above my family, but in attempting to serve my people, I found that I was prevented from fulfilling my obligations as a son, a brother, a father and a husband.' Evelyn, for one, can vouch for Mandela's admission that - 'The struggle is my life.'

Several months after the divorce, he met Winnie Nomzamo. Mandela's second marriage would face many of the same problems that had afflicted his first, but in Winnie he found a partner content to share his political sacrifice. However, in later years the actions of his outspoken wife would come back to haunt him.

As far as the government was concerned, Mandela was living up to his tribal name - 'troublemaker'. In 1961, four years after the trial began, Mandela and his co-defendants were acquitted. The trial was a major factor in the growth of the international anti-apartheid movement. Mandela's stirring defence statements had captured the public imagination both at home and abroad - he had proved himself an articulate spokesman as well as a natural leader.

In the heightening political situation, the ANC hierarchy decided that Mandela would best serve the struggle if he went into hiding. He had become their chief political prize-fighter, widely respected throughout the organisation, especially through his work with the youth wing. He knew his dedication was essential to the ANC's fight for freedom and equality, and he was determined not let his colleagues down. The national press labelled the elusive Mandela 'The Black Pimpernel'. A cult figure, famed for his dissidence, he knew that he was the government's prime target. Oliver Tambo, remembered the part Mandela played during this era, as a figurehead of the struggle, and a focus for the masses: 'He left his home, our office, his wife and children, to live the life of a political outlaw. Here began the legend of the 'Black Pimpernel'. He lived in hiding, meeting only his closest political associates, travelling round the country in disguise, popping up here to lead and advise, disappearing again when the hunt got too hot.'

However, once again, the ANC had greatly underestimated the power and recalcitrance of the apartheid regime. It would be a lifetime before Mandela would reap the rewards of his tireless devotion. With no headway being gained through mass protest, and with more repressive legislation being implemented all the time, ANC activists began to feel a deepening sense of frustration. They looked back over their thirty-year history to reach the pessimistic conclusion that their power had actually weakened. Perhaps a new approach was needed.

It was decided that a small group should lead an armed campaign against the regime. Mandela felt that their peaceful opposition could not bring about the changes needed. He realised that action was also necessary due to the possibility that the frustration and anger of the black population could erupt into civil war - Mandela hoped to harness this anger and control its eruption. In 1964, he explained: 'We believed that as a result of government policy, violence by the African people had become inevitable, and that unless responsible leadership was given to channel and control the feelings of our people, there would be outbreaks of terrorism which would produce an intensity of bitterness and hostility between the various races of this country which is not produced even by war. Secondly, we felt that without violence there would be no way open to the African people to succeed in their struggle against white supremacy...we were placed in a position in which we had to either accept a permanent state of inferiority, or to defy the Government. We chose to defy the law.'

'The Spear of the Nation' was set up as the armed wing of the ANC. Mandela, as Commander in Chief, planned to use sabotage as a way to force the government's hand. ANC literature recorded this change from peaceful protest to armed resistance: 'The time comes in the life of any nation when there remain only two choices - submit or fight. That time has come in South Africa. We shall not submit and we have no choice but to hit back by all means within our power in defence of our people, our future, and our freedom.'

Mandela felt it necessary to leave the country to undertake military training in guerrilla warfare. He travelled to Europe where he received funds and support from a number of liberal groups. It was a mark of his standing that on both continents, political leaders received him with warmth rather than caution. That, to this day, Mandela remains unblemished with the controversy that has dogged so many other armed political struggles, speaks volumes both of his principled approach, as well as the degree to which his enemy was viewed as the principle aggressor.

On his return to the country, in 1962, Mandela was captured and arrested. For the authorities, the constant police surveillance and harassment of his family and colleagues had finally paid off. (There is evidence that the South African security forces were tipped off as to his whereabouts by the CIA.) He was locked in a Johannesburg prison to await charges.

With hindsight, Mandela admitted that he had been brash and overconfident upon his return. He had been caught up in his own myth, becoming amateurish in his behaviour. It seems that Mandela relished his infamy with the white regime as much as he enjoyed his fame and power within the ANC. He realised that he had put himself and other members at risk by living dangerously and by keeping notebooks that could be used to incriminate others. 'In truth, I had been imprudent about maintaining the secrecy of my movements... It was a wonder in fact that I wasn't captured sooner.'

He was subsequently sentenced to five years in prison for inciting the public and for leaving the country without the proper documentation. These were minor charges compared to what the authorities had in mind, but they had little evidence to link him with acts of sabotage. However, a few months later, a government raid on the ANC's (once) secret headquarters caught its leaders unprepared. From the box load of evidence gathered, Mandela was implicated in attacks on the government. He was one of eleven activists charged with sabotage.

The Rivonia Trial began in 1963. Knowing that it would be relayed to the democratic world, Mandela and his fellow defendants saw the trial as an opportunity to attack the government. In court, he was at his defiant, uncompromising best - wearing traditional clothes and conducting his own defence. However, all his oratorical skills could not sway the judges. Again, Mandela faced up the stark facts of his situation: 'I was prepared for the death penalty...To be truly prepared for something, one must actually expect it... We were all prepared, not because we were brave but because we were realistic.'

In the event, and under the powerful lens of international scrutiny, the sentence was commuted to life imprisonment. Their lives had been spared but it was still a crushing blow both personally and politically. In South Africa, a life sentence literally meant just that, without any prospect of parole. Yet, world opinion was firmly behind Mandela and his fellow convicts - politicians and newspapers across the globe spoke out in their favour. The New York Times reflected this consensus, stating - 'To most of the world, these men are heroes and freedom fighters. The George Washingtons and Ben Franklins of South Africa.'

Imprisoned on Robben Island, Mandela may have felt a sense of deja vu. Not only had he been imprisoned on the island before, but as a child, he had listened to his tribal leaders narrate stories of the great chiefs incarcerated here for courageously battling against colonial rule. Many of his heroes had been jailed on the island, but none had left it alive. It seemed probable that Mandela would suffer the same fate.

Mandela's close friend, Oliver Tambo, had been more fortunate; he was smuggled out of the country before the arrests. Yet, he was left an isolated and dejected figure, unable to contact his ANC friends within South Africa. Nevertheless, he attempted to keep attention focused on the imprisoned leaders, paying special tribute to Mandela - 'As a man, Nelson is passionate, emotional, sensitive, quickly stung to bitterness and retaliation by insult and patronage. He has a natural air of authority. He cannot help magnetising the crowd...He is dedicated and fearless. He is the born mass leader.' But kind words could not change South Africa.

Mandela and the other prisoners were now isolated from the outside world. The government banned ANC literature, information regarding the prisoners, even pictures of Mandela. This strategic blackout by the government had the desired effect. In the following years, their personal sacrifice would slowly be forgotten, and for many their plight was seen as a lost cause.

In jail, the political prisoners were not respected as such, or given certain privileges; in fact, they were classed as the worst kind of criminal and were constantly harassed and humiliated. Mandela and his fellow inmates reacted to this treatment by committing themselves to a series of hunger strikes. Punishments were harsh: one of the hardest aspects of prison life, for Mandela, were the frequent spells in total isolation: 'I found solitary confinement the most forbidding aspect of prison life. There is no end and no beginning; there is only one's mind, which can play tricks. Was it a dream or did it really happen? One begins to question everything. Did I make the right decision, was my sacrifice worth it? In solitary, there is no distraction from these haunting questions.'

Such punishments were used to break a prisoner's spirit; but, as he shown throughout his life, Mandela did not lack will power. He established himself as spokesman for the political prisoners, in their dealings with the prison authorities. Over the years, even the authorities were forced to accord Mandela some of the respect his authority demanded. As a result, he gained a number of concessions for his fellow inmates, including equal food, clothing and recreation time.

If prison was not hard enough, the outside world also dealt Mandela some cruel cards. In the early 1960s, he suffered three tragedies within his family. These events were exacerbated by his inability to comfort his loved ones at times of crisis. The first tragedy was the death of his mother: Mandela received a one-line telegram, which bluntly notified him of the occurrence. This loss was compounded by the authorities' denial of his humble request to attend her funeral. In the same year, his wife Winnie was arrested and placed in prison. She was on remand for several months before her eventual release. The third tragedy took place only a short time after his mother had died. Again Mandela received a short telegram which told him of the death of his first son, Thembu, from a motor accident. In another heartless display, the authorities denied Mandela leave to prepare the funeral. For a while the prisoner became reclusive as he sought to control his emotions.

For some time, the fate of the political prisoners was forgotten by the media and the public at large. Without its gallant leaders, the antiapartheid movement had ebbed away. The spark that rekindled the flames was, ironically, of the repressive regime's own making. In June, 1976, police and security forces left sixty-nine schoolchildren dead and hundreds injured, after a protest in Soweto. The Soweto Massacre led to mass revolt throughout the townships. The world could look away no longer. The impassioned cries of 'Free Mandela' were heard again, as the convicted 'terrorist' resurfaced as the public symbol of the fight against oppression.

Throughout the next two decades, political and social unrest spread throughout South Africa. The police and security forces were becoming ever more brutal against the growing calls for reform, while different sections of the black population, in particular Xhosa and Zulu, fought against each other. As the ANC had feared, the country was teetering towards civil war. But this, of course, was also a very real threat to the government, who were finding it difficult to contain the violence, while also suffering with trade embargoes from abroad (due to its immensely unpopular system of apartheid). World opinion was clearly against the faltering regime, which began to see that political change was its only means of survival.

During the 1980s, Mandela had taken it upon himself to attempt some form of dialogue with the South African President, P.W. Botha. Both men realised that the continuing violence was raging into a state of anarchy. Mandela risked his image - his discreet liaison could well have been misinterpreted as collusion. As usual, his decision was both brave and long-sighted. He reasoned: 'There are times when a leader must move out ahead of the flock, go off in a new direction, confident that he is leading his people the right way.'

In August 1989, President Botha resigned. Mandela hoped his dialogue with the regime would not be overlooked. In an unexpected move, the new President - F.W. De Klerk - decided to continue the talks. During the meetings, Mandela lobbied for the release of his fellow activists. He achieved this aim to the point where he was the only prisoner from the Rivonia Trial still incarcerated. Out of principle, he refused to leave prison until the government removed the ban on the ANC and made steps toward the end of apartheid. Freedom, to Mandela, was more than a matter of his personal liberty.

After spending over twenty-seven years in prison, Mandela was finally released on February 11, 1990. He had convinced the government that only change to the political system would bring peace to the country. The event was marked by celebrations across the world. At the age of 72, he was once again able to publicly campaign for the abolishment of apartheid. The following year he became President of the ANC. He continued to work with President F.W. De Klerk, in order to secure universal elections in South Africa. In recognition of their hard work and mutual sacrifice, both men were awarded the Nobel Peace Prize the following year.

At last, Mandela was reaping the rewards of his life-long commitment to freedom. He was able to cast his vote in his country's first general election open to all races. The result of the ballot was no less significant for all its inevitability. On May 10, 1994, Mandela was inaugurated as the first black President of South Africa. He knew this was just another milestone in his struggle - it was now his responsibility to secure the fragile peace, as well as act against the poverty and inequality ingrained in his society.

Behind the public jubilation, Mandela faced a number of personal tribulations. The most notable of these was the crumbling relationship with Winnie. The heavy burden of Winnie's excesses (including her well-known love affairs) had placed an intolerable strain on the marriage, but at the same time he felt indebted to her personal sacrifice. In some ways, he blamed himself: 'She married a man who soon left her; that man became a myth: and the myth returned home and proved to be just a man after all.' Mandela's humble and forgiving nature was over-charitable.

Throughout the 1980s, Winnie had gained notoriety from her links with a criminal gang (who hid behind the name of Mandela FC). She was a powerful figure in the townships, both revered and feared by those involved with her. The self-styled 'mother of the nation' was, in effect, a warlord within the townships. She had been arrested on numerous occasions for suspected participation in organised crime. In 1991, she was convicted for kidnap and assault, and faced five years in prison. Her role in the much-publicised trial concerning the death of young Stompie Seipei came under the spotlight when witnesses admitted they had lied to protect her. They also testified that she had physically led the beating in which Stompie was killed. During the trial she was also incriminated in several other murders.

Mandela, in the face of compelling evidence, stuck by his estranged wife. His loyalty was unwavering. Nevertheless, he had no choice but to accept that there were now irreconcilable differences that could never be bridged. It is ironic that after twenty-seven years in Prison, Mandela commented that the time he spent with his wife after his release 'had been the loneliest of my life.'

But there was to be happiness for Mandela. In 1997, he married Graca Machell, the widow of the former President of Mozambique.

Mandela's most controversial act as President, so far, has been to mastermind the Truth and Reconciliation Commission, which aimed to establish an understanding of the crimes committed during the apartheid era. The findings from the report were published in late 1998 amid threats of legal action from both the ANC and Nationalist party. The report was criticised because it implicated both sides in crimes against humanity. The British Independent newspaper commented that 'In search of the truth the TRC has pleased no one. The right claims that it was a witch-hunt against the Afrikaner, while a furious ANC [accuses] the TRC of 'criminalising' the liberation movements struggle against apartheid.'

Mandela had hoped that by establishing a clear view of the past, the country could move forward. Unfortunately, the report seems to have opened old wounds. Despite the commission being founded on the most honourable of intentions, the country has found it simply too early to forgive and forget.

Mandela let it be known that he would not run for a second term as President, in 1999. One can only hope that South Africa can survive without the unifying force of its inspirational leader. Nelson Mandela's greatness rested upon his principled and unyielding dedication to political freedom. Yet, what was truly remarkable was his ability to forgive those who inflicted such pain upon himself and his people. It is this seminal example that can pave the way forward for a nation with so many troubles and so much potential.

Mandela retired from political life in June 1999. However, he found the seclusion difficult and he reverted to a busy public life with a daily programme of tasks, meeting with world leaders and celebrities, and worked with the Nelson Mandela Foundation in Johannesburg which was founded in 1999. The foundation focussed on rural development, school construction, and combating the spread of AIDS.

In June 2004, aged 85 and with his health failing, Mandela announced that he was "retiring from retirement" and retreated from all public life, declaring "Don't call me, I will call you." The Foundation discouraged invitations for him to appear at public events and denied most interview requests. Mandela's 90th birthday was marked across the country on 18 July 2008, with the main celebrations held at Qunu and a concert in his honour in Hyde Park, London. In a speech marking the event, Mandela called for the rich to help the poor across the world.

In 2004, Mandela successfully campaigned for the 2010 FIFA World Cup to come to South Africa, declaring that there would be "few better gifts for us in the year" marking the decade since the fall of apartheid. Mandela raised the FIFA World Cup Trophy after the World Cup was awarded to South Africa. He maintained a low profile during the event due to his ill-health. However, he made his final public appearance during the closing ceremony, where he received a warm and rapturous reception.

In February 2011, he was hospitalised with a respiratory infection before being re-hospitalised for a lung infection and gallstone removal in December 2012. A year later after suffering from a prolonged respiratory infection, Nelson Mandela died on 5 December 2013 at the age of 95. Announcing the news on South African national TV, President Jacob Zuma said Mr Mandela was at peace. "Our nation has lost its greatest son," Mr Zuma said. On 6 December 2013, Zuma announced a national mourning period of ten days. Mandela's body lay in state from 11–13th December at the Union Buildings in Pretoria and a state funeral was held on 15 December 2013 in Qunu.

Upon his death, US President Obama said, "He achieved more than could be expected of any man and today he's gone home. We've lost one of the most influential, courageous and profoundly good human beings that any of us will ever share time with on this earth. He no longer belongs to us. He belongs to the ages." Ex-US president Bill Clinton added, "Today the world has lost one of its most important leaders and one of its finest human beings. History will remember Nelson Mandela as a champion for human dignity and freedom, for peace and reconciliation."

STEVEN SPIELBERG
1946 - PRESENT DAY

For the last two decades, Steven Spielberg has enchanted world-wide audiences with his films. More than a billion people have been touched by his work. Hits such as Jaws, ET, Schindler's List and Jurassic Park, in addition to numerous business interests, have pushed his personal fortune close to $2 billion. He has built a business empire upon a childhood dream of making captivating movies. Spielberg is a self taught cinematic genius who has revolutionised the film industry.

Steven Spielberg was born on 18 December 1946 to a 'raucous' Jewish family based in Cincinnati, Ohio. In his father's bid to find employment, the family was forced to uproot on a constant basis. The first major move was to New Jersey in 1950; three years later, and with the addition of three daughters, the Spielbergs relocated to a small town outside Phoenix, Arizona.

The birth of television and its growth as a popular medium coincided with Spielberg's early childhood. His first memories recollect his immersion within the voices of the transistor radio and the images of the 'bright box'. A fascination with the new technology was passed from father to son. Arnold Spielberg had been in the Air-Force during the Second World War, but during his son's formative years was a computer engineer. Spielberg later described his father as a 'workaholic' who would always leave early for work and return late at night. However, his return would often yield a new gadget for his son to examine. As an avid science-fiction fan, Arnold Spielberg's influence on his son went deeper than a serious work ethic.

While residing in Arizona, Spielberg began to experiment with the family film camera. As his skills developed, he

45

began to work on a number of short films. Aged twelve his first film, Gunsmog (based on the classic western television series, Gunsmoke) was screened for the local Boy Scouts group. In his first three years at high school, the budding director completed fifteen short films, many of them screened for his fellow pupils. An interest was turning into an obsession.

The disintegration of his parents' marriage had a profound effect on Spielberg. The themes of familial dysfunction have been carried over into a great many of his most successful features. In Close Encounters Of The Third Kind, the leading character leaves his wife and child to commune with aliens; in Indiana Jones And The Last Crusade, Jones senior (Sean Connery) and Jones junior (Harrison Ford) spend much of the film bickering over lingering family disputes. Spielberg once described his own childhood as 'unhappy and rootless'. He gained an 'outcast attitude'. In the opinion of his biographer, John Baxter; 'He turned to television as his emotional stimulation. It became his educational medium and security blanket. For him, as for many of his contemporaries who became directors in the 70s and 80s, TV was film school.' Spielberg was never an exceptional high school student, and his new found talent drew him further in his own direction.

At the age of fourteen, his forty minute war film Escape to Nowhere won a prize at the Canyon Film Festival. In 1962, he was inspired by the epic Lawrence of Arabia; if he had any doubts as to his future vocation, this masterpiece put an end to them. He began work on his first feature film, Fireflight. Ever resourceful, Spielberg filmed in a local hospital and persuaded the local airport to close a runway while he shot a scene. Working feverishly at weekends the film took a year to complete. With a $300 loan from his father, it premiered at a local cinema. By the end of the screening, the seventeen year-old had made a $100 profit for his father. Even at this stage his films made economic, as well as artistic, sense.

Film making was becoming a way of life. He had discovered something he was conspicuously good at. For the first time he was truly in control. He also achieved a level of popularity that was usually out of the reach of 'shy, awkward looking, spotty nerds who get picked on by football jocks,' as he was later to describe himself. He increased his school profile by filming classmates and renting out movies. He was, in short, emerging from the constraints of an unhappy childhood.

When Spielberg left high school, he became eligible for the civilian draft to the Vietnam War. He realised that without a student exemption his movie-making days would almost certainly be over. He applied twice to USC Cinema School but was turned down due to poor high school grades. With this cloud hanging over him, he enrolled on an English course at the California State College, Long Beach. Although more institutionalised education was not high on his agenda, at least he was alive to pursue his real interests. The fact that he could not attend an accredited film school (unlike his peers Martin Scorsese, Francis Ford Coppola and George Lucas) did little to dent his enthusiasm.

In the summer of '67, the ambitious student sneaked into the famous Universal Studios in Los Angeles. Armed with his new found self-belief and long held desire to establish himself in the film industry, he concluded that it was time to 'up the stakes'. With a scarcely believable display of nerve he settled himself into a vacant room within the studio and simply pretended to work there as a director. He believed that from this position he would be able to net-work his way into a job. He even took the trouble of putting his name on the door and giving the main receptionist his room telephone number. Over the next few weeks he realised that his plan was unlikely to launch him into stardom. He received not a single phone call and abandoned his temporary office. The ludicrous plot had clearly failed; but what this incident does reveal is the sheer determination and positive thinking that would eventually take Spielberg to the top.

In 1968, while mixing with students in Long Beach, he became acquainted with the millionaire, Dennis Hoffman. It was a chance meeting that resulted in Hoffman funding the fledgling director's next film. Amblin, a twenty-five minute film, was the end result of this acquaintance. In the same year a Universal Studio executive, Sidney Jay Sheinberg, saw the film. Obviously impressed, he offered Spielberg a job as Producer and Director for the studio. The recipient eagerly signed a seven year contract, affectionately known within the industry as 'the Death Pact'. As John Baxter explained, 'Only the desperate - or the desperately ambitious - would sign it, and Spielberg was both.' This was the break Spielberg had been waiting for, and luck had played a leading role.

Spielberg had made his mark at last. Yet, one thought still troubled him. He longed to fulfil his childhood dream of completing his first feature film by the age of twenty one. This was not going to happen, so he re-wrote history. From then on, Spielberg perpetuated the myth that he had been born in 1947 rather than 1946. Easy. He would just delete a year of his life and become twenty one again. To a movie director anything is possible, even time-travel.

When Spielberg began his contract with Universal, he expected his career to rocket. Yet, he had to wait a number of months before a real opportunity arose. When it did, he cursed his luck. He was to direct one episode of the TV series Night Gallery. The star of the show was the ageing actress Joan Crawford, known for her on-set mood swings and temper-tantrums. He found the resulting shoot so stressful that by its conclusion he saw no option but to resign. He explained that the work was just too hard for him. One thing was certain: the life of a professional director would be very different to that of the teenage moviemaker.

For a brief period in his life, he had lost faith in his ability. Yet, it was not in his nature to merely give-in. He returned shortly afterwards with restored confidence and an insatiable hunger for the big time. The TV shows he made over the next year received encouraging reviews. His resilience would not allow a bad experience to derail his dream.

His first major success was the feature film, Duel. The screenplay found its way to Spielberg after passing through the hands of numerous producers. Fortunately, it found its way to a friend in the studio mailroom who dutifully passed it on to him. Spielberg was immediately convinced he had found suitable material for a full-scale cinematic debut. He took the idea to his executives, who had other plans for the project. Unimpressed by their reaction, he took his ideas to his original employer, Sidney Sheinberg. He bowed to Spielberg's wish but only on condition that a major star would take the lead. The project then found its way to Barry Diller, of ABC TV. Diller liked the idea and was especially pleased that a young director he much admired was in charge. Despite the absence of a star name, production went ahead.

Spielberg was disappointed to learn that his film would not get a general release. Instead, it was sold to NBC who placed it in their 'World Premiere Movie' section. When it screened in November 1971, its director finally received the widespread praise and admiration he craved. Two years later, he completed his second movie, Sugarland Express, which signalled even greater things to come. Following these successes, his future was secure. The first opportunity to direct a high-profile movie for general release arrived in 1975. The result was the unforgettable Jaws. By the end of its run it had become the highest grossing movie in history. The tale of the Great White shark established its director as Hollywood's hottest property; and left countless viewers too scared to take a bath (let alone go for a swim).

In the following years, he would fulfil even the wildest expectations, making films that mesmerised audiences while smashing box office records. Jaws has been credited with creating the phenomenon that is the 'summer Blockbuster'- films usually aimed at the youth market, providing visual, rather than intellectual, stimulation. Together with long time ally, George Lucas (creator of the Star Wars trilogy);

Spielberg became the undisputed king of the box office with such smash hits as Close Encounters, Raiders of the Lost Ark and ET. The latter was the most successful film ever, until it was superseded by Jurassic Park - another Spielberg hit.

In 1981, he learnt a valuable lesson from Lucas. A director who chose to claim a percentage of a successful film's profits, instead of a set fee, was liable to make a lot of money. The million dollars he received for Close Encounters in 1977, would seem like loose change by the mid '80s when he could command twenty percent of studio receipts. If he also produced the film his percentage would shoot up to fifty percent. By 1984, he had formed his own production company, Amblin Entertainment. MCA bought a $3.5 million office at Universal Studios for the hot-shot director. A string of hits followed, including The Colour Purple, the Indiana Jones trilogy and Empire of the Sun.

Spielberg was not only directing, but also wearing the cap of Producer and Executive Producer. He was involved with such successes as Back To The Future, Who Framed Roger Rabbit and Gremlins. He also made it his business to nurture a new group of budding directors through the ranks of Hollywood, people who shared his own love of film. The company also expanded into the highly profitable arena of TV animation, achieving great success with Tiny Toons Adventures and Animaniacs, both of which were modelled on the manic style of the early Warner Brothers cartoons. A year after its foundation, Amblin was making in excess of $50 million a year. Spielberg had become the most successful director and producer in American film history. Baseline's Encyclopaedia of Film reasoned that his astonishing achievements rested on an 'uncanny knack for eliciting and manipulating audience response.'

During this period of almost unfettered success, there were certain notable failures - personal and professional. In 1979, Spielberg decided to flex his creative muscles and create a big budget, all star comedy. The result was 1941, the only Spielberg film that has bombed both commercially and critically. It was brash, over the top and sadly lacking in laughs. On a more private level, Spielberg's four year marriage to actress Amy Irving ended in 1989. In October 1991, Spielberg married actress Kate Capshaw.

By the late Eighties and early Nineties, Spielberg's position as king of Hollywood was unassailable. Yet, rather than resting on his laurels, he sought to build on his achievements. The films Schindler's List and Jurassic Park illustrated Spielberg's need to both innovate and consolidate. In term of narrative, Jurassic Park was predictable fare dubbed 'Jaws with claws' by the critics. But its incredible special effects and rollercoaster pacing made it the most successful film of all time (at least until the all conquering Titanic took the spotlight). Utilising unprecedented technology, Spielberg brought incredibly life-like dinosaurs to big screen, delighting viewers of all ages. The film grossed over $950 million, of which Spielberg pocketed around a third.

Schindler's List, a frank and intensely moving portrayal of the Holocaust, became its maker's most critically lauded production to date, landing nearly every major industry award including seven Oscars (Best Picture and Best Director amongst them). After many years of commercial success had failed to deliver the ultimate accolade, Spielberg must have wondered if he would always be snubbed by the Oscar Committee. But here, finally, was validation for Spielberg the artist.

Although Spielberg is the most lucrative filmmaker on the planet, a desire to create something more meaningful seems to have superseded commercial interests. Throughout his career, Spielberg has never been viewed in the same light as the more critically acclaimed directors of his generation, such as Martin Scorsese and Francis Ford Coppola. While they made the films they wanted to make, based on their unique artistic sensibilities, Spielberg deployed a more populist approach. However, over the last five years, three of the four films he has directed, have been serious, even controversial, adult-orientated dramas. Schindler's List; Amistad, the historical slave drama; and Saving Private

Ryan, an unbearably visceral World War II movie, all seem far removed from earlier and more light-weight efforts. This apparent aim to extend the boundaries of his own considerable talents, illustrates that even after so many successful years, Spielberg's energy and enthusiasm have not diminished.

The year 1994 proved to be a milestone for both Spielberg and the movie industry; an historic alliance was drawn up by Spielberg, the music producer David Geffen and the former Disney executive, Jeffrey Katzenberg. Three of the most powerful figures in the entertainment business, they joined forces to form 'DreamWorks SKG' the first major new Hollywood studio since Twentieth Century Fox was established in 1935. DreamWorks gave Spielberg greater financial clout and artistic control than ever before. Such is the esteem in which he is held by his two colleagues, that Geffen once quipped to Katzenberg, 'We ought to call this new company the Spielberg Brothers ... Anything Steven thinks is important, we want to invest in.'

DreamWorks initial output has been variable, to say the least. It's first cinematic release The Peacemaker and two television series, failed to make the grade either financially or critically. Affairs were set straight by the world-wide success of Saving Private Ryan - which has taken over $200 million dollars. The future looks bright for the studio with the groundbreaking animated feature Antz and a fourth Indiana Jones film in the pipeline.

This was just one of Spielberg's many ventures. He also set up a partnership with the computer games manufacturer Sega, and is involved in a joint-project with Microsoft, contributing to the advancement of online games. As well as these, he is also co-owner of a 'deep sea diner' called 'Dive'- a $7 million restaurant which specialises in over twenty kinds of submarine sandwiches.

On a more personal level, Spielberg has ploughed money into a project to compile a video history of over 41,000 Holocaust survivors, and has donated over $85 million to support and preserve Jewish culture and education. Obviously this is a cause close to the director's heart, as the emotional force of Schindler's List, his most accomplished work, testifies.

His fame and wealth have come at a price. This year, 1998, saw Spielberg in court to testify against a stalker who had been plaguing him for a number of years. The stalker was sentenced to 25 years for attempting to kidnap the wealthy director. As well as this vile intrusion into his private life, two recent projects (Amistad and Twister) were hit with charges of plagiarism. Spielberg was exonerated of any wrong doing; but some believe that Spielberg and DreamWorks are skating on thin ice, that only their wealth and influence have precluded big payouts and further law suits.

With eight of the highest grossing films in history, Spielberg's reputation as the world's most successful film director is assured. The capacity to tune into the imagination of all age-groups is a priceless gift of which he has taken full advantage. His life-long love affair with cinema, which began in his formative years, has never waned. Allied to this natural enthusiasm, an unfaltering business sense has proved equally significant. Once asked to account for his own success, he replied: 'The process for me is mostly intuitive... There are films that I feel that I need to make, for a variety of reasons, for personal reasons, for reasons that I want to have fun, that the subject matter is cool, that I think my kids will like it. And sometimes I just think that it will make a lot of money.'

STEPHEN HAWKING
1942 - PRESENT DAY

Stephen Hawking likes to play down his illness. Yet, to be told at the age of twenty one that you have only two years to live, is likely to be the turning point of any life, no matter how intelligent or determined the individual. The image of the wheelchair bound genius, a shining intellect cloaked behind a withered body and computer-generated voice, is central to the world's fascination. But the scientist dubbed the 'new Einstein' has more to offer than an engaging media image. His research into black holes and the birth of the Universe has inspired an audience well beyond the scientific community. His ground-breaking book, A Brief History of Time, has sold over 10 million copies, proving that its author's appeal is truly universal.

Isobel and Frank Hawking chose Oxford for a good reason. Amid the chaos of war-time Britain they had found a haven for the birth of their first child. Nazi Germany had promised not to bomb Oxford and Cambridge on condition that its own university cities of Heidelberg and Gottigen would be spared. In this academic sanctuary, Stephen Hawking was born on 8 January 1942, 300 years to the day after Galileo's death. This coincidence was almost rendered insignificant. Weeks after the birth, on return to their native north London, a V2 rocket nearly put an end to the young family. Fortunately they were out at the time the missile devastated a neighbouring house. Hawking's fragile life would encounter many such near misses.

The Hawkings were a colourful family, to say the least. Their house in St Albans, Hertfordshire - where they moved in 1950 - mirrored the eccentricity. Plaster crumbled, wallpaper peeled, and amid the disrepair were strewn books and paintings. As Stephen grew up, his room became cluttered with exercise books, electrical contraptions and various other half-completed inventions. The family car was a London taxi - replaced by a Ford only when the family set out on a year-long driving tour of India. Needless to say, this was not a typical 1950s family outing. Unfortunately, Stephen had to miss out on the adventure, as nothing could be allowed to hinder his education. His father, a specialist in tropical diseases, was keen for Stephen to pursue a medical career. The son had ideas of his own.

A shy, stammering, rather feeble schoolboy enrolled at the private St Albans School in 1952. The school boasted a proud academic heritage - although not quite as proud as that of Frank Hawking's first choice - the prestigious Westminster School. The sickly child had failed to live up to his father's ambition by being ill on the day of the entrance exam. Young Hawking was bright, earning his place in the top sets and mixing with the smartest students, yet not exceptional, and certainly not marked out for greatness. In fact, it would have been easy to overlook the embryonic genius as he eked out his school days, attempting to avoid the bullies and side-step the rigmarole of physical games. Unsurprisingly, the slight and slightly eccentric schoolboy was no athlete. Yet, in retrospect, there were early clues to Hawking's brilliant future.

There was another side to the awkward figure, whose jabbering speech was mockingly dubbed 'Hawkingese'. He was fascinated by the way things worked, as the piles of electronic litter in his room testified. (The hapless inventor once received a 500 volt shock, attempting to manufacture an amplifier from an old television.) Another hobby was devising the rules to intricate board games he would play with his brainy friends, although these were often so complex it would take a whole day to explain them. Yet, in one respect Hawking was strikingly superior to those around him. As his close-knit band of friends began to concern themselves with religion, the occult and extrasensory perception (ESP), he stood back as a peripheral and rather sceptical character. His rationalist mentality refused to be cajoled along with the others. A friend, Michael Church, told the Independent newspaper of an encounter with Hawking in his 'cluttered, joke-inventor's den. Our talk turned to the meaning of life - a topic I felt pretty hot on at the time - when suddenly I was arrested by an awful realization that he was encouraging me to make a fool of myself and watching me from a great height. It was a profoundly unnerving moment.'

Hawking sailed through his school exams. By the sixth-form he had established himself as a promising student, able to attain the best grades with negligible effort. Father and son were united in the choice of Oxford University and disunited in the choice of degree. With a famed stubbornness Hawking stood his ground, dismissing the virtues of the medical profession in favour of natural science (mathematics and physics). After stunning results in the usually daunting entrance exam, he was offered a scholarship to University College, where his father had studied.

A seventeen-year-old Hawking arrived at Oxford in 1959. The bright young undergraduate had made it. With his new found independence and all the resources of a world-famous seat of learning at his disposal, he should have had the time of his life. He didn't. His first year was marked by a consuming boredom that verged on depression. The course was too easy, he effortlessly solved problems that caused other students numerous sleepless nights. He soon turned his attention to correcting his textbooks. He later estimated that over his three years at Oxford, he had worked on average less than a hour a day. however, without his school-friends he felt isolated and dejected, spending long evenings drinking alone in his room.

A transformed Stephen Hawking returned to Oxford after the first year. His academic attitude was the same: a blasé brilliance which sometimes bordered on arrogance. But socially he was a different person: popular, boisterous, active. He even became involved in sport, taking up rowing. His light frame was hardly suited to the physical aspect of the sport, but was ideal for the position of cox. Perched at the end of the boat, barking instructions to the perspiring crew, Hawking had found an interest outside physics and science fiction (which he read voraciously). He gained a reputation as a somewhat reckless navigator, returning battered vessels with vague and unconvincing excuses. He was committed to the rowing club without taking the sport too seriously, and while ensuring he took full advantage of the benefits to his social life. When old school friends caught up with Hawking they scarcely recognized their once introverted chum.

Hawking had displayed the adroitness to adapt to circumstances, an ability which would face a far tougher test in the near future. By his final year at Oxford, he was already beginning to suffer from an odd clumsiness; more than once he had fallen down stairs and was also having problems tying his shoelaces. But, for the moment, he was content to dismiss these distractions, more pressing concerns were approaching. He decided to apply for a PhD at Cambridge to study cosmology under the eminent British astronomer, Fred Hoyle. All he needed was a first, a formality for a student of Hawking's calibre, or so it would seem. But it was not unknown for such a high-flier to develop intellectual vertigo at the last moment. In the event, the unthinkable happened. He spent a sleepless night before his finals and botched some of his answers. The result was a borderline grade. Thankfully, he was afforded an interview with the examiners in which he could exhibit his prodigious brain-power. Declared Hawking: 'If I get a first I shall go to Cambridge. If I receive a second I will remain at Oxford. So I expect that you will give me a first.' As usual he got his way and headed for Cambridge.

Hawking's 1962 arrival at Trinity College, Cambridge was as disappointing as his initiation into Oxford. Instead of world-famous Hoyle, he was to be tutored by Dennis Sciama. In time, this would prove far from regrettable, as Sciama would go out of his way to assist the talented graduate. But for now, it was seen as a set-back. Other problems accumulated: Hawking could not find a suitable research project, furthermore, due to his lackadaisical attitude at Oxford, he had not studied maths to the appropriate level and was finding difficulty in coming to terms with the subject. Yet these problems, serious though they were, would soon be put into harsh perspective.

At Christmas vacation the same year, Hawking's parents were concerned with their son's health and insisted that he should visit a doctor. A referral to a specialist led to comprehensive medical tests. When the results arrived the family were stunned; Stephen was devastated. He had contracted amyotrophic lateral sclerosis (ALS), commonly known in Britain as motor neuron disease, and in the US as Lou Gehrig's disease. The incurable muscle-wasting condition sentences the sufferer to a progressively vegetative state. The creeping paralysis leads to death by suffocation or pneumonia. Yet, while the body degenerates the brain is left untouched. Hawking learned of his fate at Cambridge; the doctors gave him two years to live. For some time he drank heavily, and the dark strains of Wagner bellowed from his room. What point was there in pursuing a PhD that would never be finished?

At a New Year party, the graduate had attracted the attentions of Jane Wilde, a young A-Level student. She went to visit Hawking in his understandably morbid and distressed state. As the relationship blossomed, the young physicist began to snap out of his torpor. As the couple planned a future together, Hawking was forced to face the world again. He began to socialize more with other PhD students at the Physics Department, gaining a renewed interest in his subject. In particular, he took an interest in the latest work of Hoyle. Hawking had access to Hoyle's work through another research student assisting the eminent scientist, and started to develop the ideas further. Hoyle was an exponent of the 'steady state' theory of the Universe - he actually coined the phrase 'Big Bang' in order to deride the idea of spontaneous creation. He chose to announce his latest findings before a meeting of the Royal Society in London. Hawking also chose the meeting as the time to make his mark. After his lecture Hoyle asked if there were any questions. Using a stick as support Hawking got to his feet: 'The quantity you're talking about diverges,' he declared. An astonished Hoyle refuted the upstart and demanded, 'How do you know?' 'Because I worked it out,' came the confident reply. The muted laughter that faced the assertive research student was shortlived. He wrote a paper to prove his findings, it was generally accepted.

As Hawking began to experience greater difficulty both speaking and walking, his academic career gathered pace. Under the guidance of his supervisor, Sciama, Hawking attended talks by a much-admired mathematician - Roger Penrose. Penrose spoke of his work on 'singularities' - points of infinite density at the core of black holes, at which space and time, along with the known laws of physics, seemed to disappear. Inspired by Penrose's ideas, Hawking was struck by the notion of applying the mathematician's work to the entire Universe. This was to prove a decisive breakthrough: at last he had a direction for his thesis. Thanks to a sparkling final chapter, this rather uneven thesis was accepted and its author became Dr Stephen Hawking. Moreover, Penrose would become a trusted friend as well as an important collaborator in Hawking's work.

Partly through stunts such as the Royal Society episode, Hawking had made a name for himself, and was awarded a fellowship at the University so he could continue his research. When he married Jane in 1965, he was already living on borrowed time. She was to become his nurse as well as wife, sacrificing her own career to support a man she knew was capable of great things. Hawking developed an incredibly positive outlook, refusing to submit to his condition. He has always demanded to be treated the same as anyone else, making only the most rudimentary concessions to his disease. At his small residence in the centre of Cambridge, he would struggle agonizingly up the stairs deploring all offers of assistance. In Jane's words, 'Some would call his attitude determination, some obstinacy. I've called it both at one time or another. I suppose that's what keeps him going.'

By the mid Sixties, the physicist's research into black holes was attracting real interest in the scientific community. He was invited to speak at a relativity meeting in Miami, although a friend had to deliver the talk as Hawking's voice had faded to a barely audible whine. The irony was not lost on Hawking - he was losing his voice just as he was finding something really big to say to the world. He also teamed up with Penrose to further investigate the puzzle of singularities. They concluded, profoundly, that if Einstein's general theory of relativity was correct, there must have been a singularity at the beginning of time.

As the decadent decade passed, Hawking swapped his stick for crutches, before finally succumbing to the necessity of a wheelchair. ALS was robbing him of mobility and the means to communicate, yet in his choice of career he had been somewhat fortunate. Theoretical physics is one of the few scientific disciplines that requires little more than brain power. If his subject had relied on physical experiment, his career would have been over. As it happens, Hawking's interest is of an ultimately speculative and theoretical nature - he has surprisingly little interest in looking through telescopes, for example. He was undoubtedly hindered by the inability to write things down, but he overcame this obstacle by sheer mental agility. He developed a way to manipulate huge complex equations in his head, and his powers of memory have often astonished his colleagues. On one occasion, at the Institute of Theoretical Astronomy (which he joined in 1968), he amazed a secretary by recalling a minute error he had made a day earlier, amid forty pages of dictated equations.

Hawking was, in fact, full of surprises. A year earlier, the first of his three children was born. As a friend, David Schramm, would announce years later to a packed lecture theatre, 'by the fact that his youngest son Timothy is less than half the age of the disease, clearly not all of Stephen is paralysed!' Many in the audience were shocked; Hawking, renowned for his sense of humour, was delighted.

For Hawking, the 1970s marked the beginning of two decades of phenomenal achievement. He had already outlived and outperformed all expectations, but the best was yet to come. His new cosmological findings would catapult Hawking from lauded academic to world celebrity. He travelled widely, completing numerous lecture tours as the accolades piled up.

At the age of 32, he was elected Fellow of the Royal Society, one of the honour's youngest recipients. In the same year, he was struck by an idea that would send tremors throughout the scientific community, and beyond. As he went through the painfully slow process of going to bed, he hit upon a new way to understand black holes. He was so excited by the breakthrough he couldn't sleep and felt compelled to telephone Penrose early next morning. By applying quantum physics to the enigma of black holes he concluded that they could emit radiation and even explode - a revolutionary notion acknowledged by the subsequent term - 'Hawking Radiation'. More revolutionary still was that he had reconciled the two major strands of twentieth century physics: quantum theory and general relativity. This was the task which Einstein had singularly failed to achieve at the end of his working life. Stephen Hawking was truly standing on the shoulders of giants.

Hawking was persuaded by his old friend, Dennis Sciama, to reveal his findings at a conference near Oxford. The slumped figure was wheeled onto the platform. The audience listened intently to the barely intelligible voice, as it delivered its radical message. Again, Hawking's work spurred a dramatic response - the conference organizer, John G Taylor, leapt from his seat, proclaimed the speech was 'nonsense' and stormed out. The findings were published in Nature as was Taylor's hastily written rebuttal. Needless to say, only one of the papers sent shockwaves around the science world, winning even greater acclaim for its author.

Soon after becoming a Fellow of the Royal Society, Hawking was invited to spend a year at the prestigious Caltech research institute in Pasadena. As his family basked in the Californian sun, Hawking made friends with some of the biggest names in science, including the famous bongo-playing physicist, Richard Feynman. He worked closely with eminent cosmologist Kip Thorne, with whom he initiated a legendary bet. Hawking wagered that Cygnus X-1 - an X-ray source in space, first discovered in the early 1970s - did not contain a black hole. If he was right he would receive a year's subscription to Private Eye, a satirical magazine; if not, Thorne would receive a year's supply of Penthouse. In 1990, Hawking admitted defeat. In typically mischievous fashion he organized a break-in to Thome's office, leaving a statement of defeat signed with a thumb-print. As promised, the dubious publication began to arrive on Thome's doormat.

The wheelchair never suited Hawking's temperament. Tired of being pushed around he upgraded to an electric version. The freewheeling physicist became a common sight around Cambridge, his reckless steering a throwback to his rowing days. In 1992, this recklessness could have cost him his life, when his motorized wheelchair was hit by a car in Cambridge city centre. He was lucky to leave the scene with only minor injuries. Yet, the wheelchair was an indispensable source of freedom, even allowing Hawking to indulge in one of his primary passions - dancing. At every possible opportunity, whether student disco or posh function, he could be found on the dance floor, his wheelchair programmed to execute any number of crazy spins. In less joyous moods he has also been known to drive over the toes of people unlucky enough to get on his wrong side. As he is keen to point out, he goes through the same emotions and mood swings as everyone else. Occasional tantrums have upset junior colleagues, yet it's probably fair to say he's more renowned for his free spirited and optimistic approach to life.

In 1978, Hawking received the prestigious Albert Einstein Award. A year later came another proud moment, he was made Lucasian Professor at Cambridge. He was thrilled to think that one of the architects of physics - Isaac Newton - had held the same position more than three hundred years earlier. Hawking had reached the age of thirty-seven, making a mockery of the doctors' prediction so many years ago. By now he was a house-hold name, with numerous TV programmes, newspaper articles and books in his honour. Hawking's own output of scientific books and papers had been equally prolific. Despite the widespread opinion that he had probably reached the pinnacle of his career, Hawking was far from finished.

The new Lucasian Professor could have used his inaugural lecture to reminisce about his inspirational career. Instead, he chose to look to the future, wowing the audience with talk of a 'unified theory of everything' - proposing that the ultimate laws of the Universe could be in reach by the end of the century. In 1981, he again courted controversy by expounding a 'no-boundary' model of the universe. If the model was correct, he said, there would be no time before the Big Bang, eliminating the need for a creator. The place he chose to reveal the theory? A conference at the Vatican. But days after the speech, when numerous guests were due to meet the Pope, many were shocked as the pontiff kneeled to be on a level with the slouched figure of Hawking, and devoted more time to the physicist than any other visitor. Around the same time he met another dignitary when the Queen presented him with a CBE.

Despite the plethora of awards, Hawking was not yet financially secure. On top of private nursing for himself, and schooling for his children, was the worry of what would happen to his family if his health deteriorated. By the early Eighties, he gave serious consideration to the idea of writing a popular science book. He fought hard to get the best possible deal from his university publishers who offered a record advance (for them) of £10,000. But Hawking was already the most famous scientist alive and could command a much higher sum in the US; Bantam Press eventually won the battle with a very lucrative package, including a $250,000 advance. Refusing a ghost-writer, but bowing to advice to leave out complex equations, he committed his precious time to the popular project.

The physicist was working on his latest draft in Geneva when his condition plummeted. His nurse was making a routine check on her patient one night when she discovered him suffering with severe breathing problems. He was rushed to the Cantonal Hospital. When Jane finally arrived from Germany, she found her husband on a life support machine, and herself facing a thankless decision. Without a tracheotomy operation - which involved a breathing device being implanted in his neck - he might not live; with it he would never make a verbal sound again. She had no choice but to condemn her husband to silence.

After the operation, Hawking returned to Cambridge. Jane was distraught, reduced to writing begging letters to safeguard her husband's future. As well as financial assistance, Hawking was sent a US computer program allowing him to construct sentences which could be vocalized through a voice-synthesizer. The process was slow, but invaluable. Hawking, as ever, saw the funny side, greeting people with, 'Hello, please excuse my American accent.' In time, a portable device was fitted to his wheelchair so he could continue to deliver lectures. After a lecture, it can take up to ten minutes for Hawking to respond to a question; on occasion, the incorrigible professor likes to delay proceedings for this time, before delighting the audience with a single-word answer.

A Brief History of Time: from the Big Bang to Black Holes, was published in 1988. Not unlike its author, it outperformed all predictions. In ten years, it had sold more than ten million copies and been translated into thirty languages. For a science book its success was unprecedented, remaining in the Sunday Times best-sellers list for a staggering 234 weeks. Some critics viewed it as the ultimate 'coffee table' book, often displayed, seldom read. Yet, that such an esoteric work could score a direct hit on the general public is an achievement in itself. Its potential to inspire a new generation of scientists is enormous; the rewards may be reaped for some time. And, as far as Hawking is concerned, suffice it to say that finance is no longer a problem.

A sad consequence of Hawking's global celebrity, was the much publicized break up of his marriage in 1990. The tabloid press wrung its hands over tales that the crippled genius had left his wife and children to move in with his long-time nurse Elaine Mason, whom he later married. To add to the scandal, she was the wife of David Mason - the computer engineer responsible for installing the portable voice synthesizer to Hawking's wheelchair. In truth, Stephen and Jane had been growing apart for years. She came to feel an appendage to the great scientist and his meteoric career, and began to pursue her own interests. That Jane was a dedicated Christian also caused friction, in view of some of her husband's sceptical remarks.

In the Nineties, Hawking took full advantage of his stardom, making a cameo appearance in an episode of Star Trek, featuring on albums by Radiohead and Pink Floyd, and earning substantial sums of money from a British Telecom commercial. Although his comments on time-travel (a theoretical possibility) and aliens, made the front pages of the press, it is probably fair to assume that his scientific legacy had already been lain. His 1997 television series, Stephen Hawking's Universe, was enthusiastically received by the public, again underlining his reputation as a great ambassador for popular science. The following year he was made Companion of Honour by the Queen. He has also lent his name and energies to a number of disabled causes.

Stephen Hawking's unparalleled intellect has won him a place in the historic procession of the great scientists. His best-selling book, A Brief History of Time, broke through the confines of the science establishment to turn the attentions of the masses to some of the longest-standing and most profound questions in human history. However, to admire the Cambridge physicist does not require an understanding of singularities, black holes or unified theories of everything. His story is a very human one; an individual obstinately refusing to give up, regardless of the obstacles thrown in his way. There is a tendency, partly due to the rather metallic voice, to regard Hawking as a purely cerebral creature, as some logical force of science. But beneath the facade there is a humour and humanity of a very different (but equally inspiring) nature.

CHRIS EVANS

1966 - PRESENT DAY

From nerdish schoolboy to millionaire TV celebrity, Chris Evans' rise to stardom has been as conspicuous as his appearance. What sort of character shifts from Tarzan-o-gram to boss of Virgin Radio? Is Evans a gifted entertainer, a shrewd businessman, a manipulative bully or all three? Either way, he has climbed to the top of his profession and beyond. His maverick career has earned him a hugely successful production company, several groundbreaking television shows and a radio station. One thing is for certain: there is more to the man than the impish character he exhibits before the television cameras.

Christopher Evans was born on April Fools' Day (1 April) 1966, in the town of Warrington. He was the youngest of three children raised in the working-class district of Orford. The youth was academically bright and possessed a cheeky sense of humour perfectly tailored to the theme of his birth date.

Any hopes of an idyllic childhood were shattered when his father died of cancer in 1979, when Evans was only thirteen years old. This loss had a fundamental effect on the impressionable teenager; it was the catalyst for a severe change. He had always been a bit of a joker, but had maintained a high standard of school work. After the death, he lost interest in school and took on a more disruptive aspect. Teachers and classmates had expected Evans to breeze into higher education, but he developed more immediate ambitions and the will to accomplish them. Psychologist Dr Bryan Tully elaborates in David Jones biography of Evans entitled Freak or Unique? : 'There is quite a lot of evidence that the loss of a parent at an early age like this can be a spur to some people (A person such as this has a strong sense of entitlement: they have suffered greatly and now they will do as they please and have the rewards they deserve.'

Evans described his father's death as 'the shotgun that started the race'. The race presumably signified a personal quest to make the most of his life, no matter what. He explained, '1 was a fourteen year old who was suddenly forced into dealing with the realities of the world. In a way, that's when my life started. I grabbed every moment of every day, I still have that attitude.' Another characteristic that Evans has carried since his early schooldays, is his unwillingness to accept defeat. One story from his youth sums this up perfectly. Glynn Povey, a friend at the time, remembers that: 'when we were nine or ten, we had a paper aeroplane contest at school and the whole class entered. Chris thought he was an ace at making paper planes and took it all deadly seriously. But I came first and he came third, he was so upset that he cried like a baby. He hated losing at anything.'

Evans strength of purpose seems to have been acquired from his mother, Minnie, who, in his own words, 'showed just how much strength it is possible for a person to have'. Armed with this obstinate will to succeed, his teenage years were littered with money-making schemes and plans to get a foot on the ladder of success. His ambitions ranged from ownership of a newsagent to becoming a radio presenter. One recurrent wish was to host the Radio One Breakfast Show. How distant a dream this must have seemed to friends and family, who had to listen to the boastful child proclaiming that one day he would be the voice behind the biggest radio show in Britain.

Evans had always been a high-spirited child, but after the loss of his father his actions became increasingly eccentric and outlandish. A striking example of this was the odd preoccupation with exposing himself to people. If the testimony of former school friends and work colleagues is to be believed, he would drop his trousers at every opportunity without the slightest hint of embarrassment or consideration for those he might offend. Courtney Gibson, who worked with Evans on The Big Breakfast television show, puts the matter bluntly: 'He didn't care who coped an eyeful of his dick...There was no sense of decorum at all.'

This was not the only questionable trait he carried from childhood into his adult years. A tendency to throw tantrums and become embroiled in bullying was also carried from the playground into the workplace. Evans' inclination to bully junior staff seems to be the direct consequence of his own experience at school. His relationship with his school peers was volatile, and his trademark ginger hair, spectacles and mischievous humour made him a prime target for childish persecution. In a 1994 interview with The Sun, he admitted: 'being a ginger kid was hell on earth. I was picked on and got into a lot of fights but didn't win a single one. When I was ten it was decided that I needed glasses and that only made things worse. Being a red haired, skinny four-eyes does you very few favours at school. I may be smiling in the pictures but I wasn't the cheeky chappy you might think.' Not for the first time, things appear to have come full circle, with Evans appropriating the role of the bully. Courtney Gibson described him as an 'aggressive, rude, mean-spirited malcontent with a profound lack of humanity and the shortest wick in show business.' His former boss, Tim Grundy agrees: 'there is a cruel streak in the way he treats people...He was just nasty to everybody, totally superior to lesser mortals like soundmen, cameramen, secretaries.' An example of this ludicrous intolerance of 'underlings' is recalled by his biographer, David Jones. Evans apparently sacked his then personal assistant for the 'criminal' offence of failing to find him a suitable helmet to match his brand new motor scooter.

However, Chris Evans was not always the overbearing boss. On his way to the top he was willing to undertake almost any job. Tarzan-o-gram, street busker, private detective; there was nothing he was too embarrassed to try. This total lack of inhibition, allied to an undeniable sense of energy and enthusiasm, can hardly be over emphasised. Ex-partner Alison Ward, confirms this frenzied eagerness: 'He fitted more into a day than other people fit into a week. He flitted and changed and tried all different things. One minute he was mad keen to do one thing, the next minute he had decided to do something else completely, only he had forgotten to tell you about it.'

Back in his mid-teens, Evans found work in a local hospital radio station as a stand-in DJ. It was a modest, but well-calculated, step toward a 'real' career break. After he won a trip to the Manchester Studios of Piccadilly Radio, his ambition gained a true focus. Capitalising on his hospital radio experience, he applied for an assistant position at Piccadilly Radio on the show of mad-cap presenter Timmy Mallet. Evans got the job, and Mallet gave him the nick-name of 'Nobby No Levels' - a reference to his marked lack of academic attainment. Mallet was to prove a huge influence. Both his zany on air style and repellent off-air temperament were appropriated by his young protégé. Tim Grundy, a DJ at the station remembers: 'He [Mallet] was cruel. He was nasty and would shout at them [his assistants] continuously - he had a lot of traits Chris Evans developed. Timmy would go into a record and he was Mr Nice, then he'd close the microphone and become Mr Nasty.' For the next few years, Evans helped out on the show, and took full advantage of any opportunity to act as stand-in presenter. As a result of his long hours spent at the radio station, Evans was sacked from his part - time job in a newsagent; his enthusiasm to own a shop had evaporated. No matter, a career in entertainment was now fully in view.

In 1985, Evans was promoted to DJ at the same station. He happily immersed himself in a hectic work-schedule. His responsibility was the notorious 'graveyard shift' - two 'til six in the morning. After this early morning slot he would remain in the studio to act as sidekick to the breakfast show DJ. He would then perform his Tarzan-o-gram routine at parties, before returning to the graveyard shift again. He gained a reputation as an ambitious workaholic; his ability to 'burn the candle at both ends' became legendary. He also began to demonstrate a flair for self-promotion which would become a trademark. Once, as a publicity stunt, he pretended to live in a tent at the bottom of a friend's garden with his pregnant girlfriend, Alison Ward. He was constantly coming up fresh ideas to promote his show.

As his popularity grew, Evans became increasingly cocky, boorish and prepared to push the limits of taste. This resulted in larger audiences but also caused problems. On one occasion he overstepped the mark, cracking a tasteless joke about a cat being micro waved, immediately after a news report concerning cruelty to animals. The phone lines at Piccadilly were jammed with complaints. Evans paid with his job. In fact, he would probably have survived if his ego had not taken exception to being reprimanded by his boss. Rather than swallow his pride, he preferred to resign. Unable to accept any authority but his own, he acted with child-like stubbornness, later confessing: 'I was a twenty-year old totally unemployable, arrogant little shit. I'd blown it in a big way.'

Despite the set-back his luck held. He moved to London, abandoning girlfriend, Alison and his new-born daughter. He landed a job with another radio station - imaginatively named 'RADIO RADIO' to help produce The Jonathan Ross Show. Evans' heart was set on presenting but he knew an opportunity when he saw one. He now had a healthy salary and the chance to work with one of the biggest names in the business, but this was not enough - he was after Ross' job. His ex-boss at the station revealed, 'He thought he could be a better presenter than Ross straightaway, and he was nagging to be given his chance the whole time.' Evans' self-belief was sky-high, and he was hungry to prove himself.

While working at the station he latched onto an idea floated at one of the regular creative meetings. It was not his idea, but he had the guile to profit from it. Several years later, it would evolve into the hit TV show Don't Forget Your Toothbrush, with none other than Chris Evans as host.

It was not long before the broadcasting heavy-weights were attracted by Evans' exuberant antics. Blind to his promise not to break his contract, he was more than happy to be poached by the BBC's Greater London Radio. His celebrity grew on the back of his two cultish GLR shows, Interference and Round at Chris's. He was still only twenty-three, but his career had really caught fire. His unique shows caught the attention of radio and TV executives desperate to sign-up the 'next big thing'.

On September 17, 1991, Evans married his producer girlfriend Carol McGiffin. The ceremony was held at a registry office and attended by neither family nor friends. They separated after a mere eight months. There were attempts at reconciliation but Chris' focus was firmly on his career. He barely had time for himself, let alone a partner. In 1993, they divorced.

A year before his marriage break-up, his boyhood dream of presenting the prestigious Radio One Breakfast Show came a significant step closer. He accepted a Saturday afternoon spot on the station, taking over from the more sedate Philip Schofield. Things did not go as smoothly as he had hoped. He had long enjoyed the creative freedom of the smaller commercial stations, but at the BBC he was expected to conform to certain standards. His old friend Johnnie Walker recalls the sense of anti-climax: 'I met him in the corridor and he said, "Johnnie, I'm so upset. All I ever wanted was to work at Radio One...and now I'm here it's completely crap." '

Evans began to realise that his obsession with his career had come at a cost. His personal life was in a mess, and behind the wacky veneer was a deep-seated insecurity. He knew he was seen by many as both arrogant and selfish. He attempted to find a remedy for his troubles in the form of a psychotherapist. The therapy focused on the impact of his father's death. As a youth, it had spurred him on to make the most of his life, but in his blinkered dash to succeed he had neglected the people around him. Once he had completed the ten week course, Evans believed he was a changed man, and for a short time his colleagues enjoyed the change too. Yet, nothing in this volatile entertainer's life stands still for very long, and soon the temper tantrums were back.

Evans' major television break arrived in the shape of Channel Four's The Big Breakfast in 1992. This hugely successful venture provided Evans with all the limelight he required. The anarchic programme firmly bore the impression of its tireless host, and he gained much of the credit when its ratings topped two million, making it one of the channel's most successful shows. In 1993, he established his own production company - Ginger Productions - and using the personal and financial clout he had accrued, he produced, directed and hosted his own television show, the phenomenally successful Don't Forget Your Toothbrush.

Yet, if the lure of television appeared to point the way forward, Evans' love-affair with radio was far from over. After an unsettled spell at Virgin Radio, he finally realised a life-long ambition. In 1995, he was hired by the new controller of Radio One, Matthew Bannister, to become presenter of The Breakfast Show. He signed a contract with the BBC giving his company £1 million to produce and present the show over an eight month period. Between April and December that year, he restored half a million listeners and a measure of confidence to the somewhat faltering station. However, his lack of responsibility was once again evident when he failed to turn up to a show in December - he'd been partying the night before. He was reprimanded but not fired, a clear sign of his standing within the Corporation. Gillian Evans of the Daily Telegraph wrote that: 'Evans doing as he pleases has become a fact of life... he, the naughty lad, who always wins has become the ultimate fantasy figure - Dennis the Menace and Sid the Sexist rolled into one, but with Lord Snooty's dosh.'

The ginger school kid had become a national celebrity, and his new found status yielded personal as well as financial rewards. After the break up of his marriage, he was linked with a succession of beautiful high profile women including high society beauty, Rachel Tatton Smith, and Kim Wilde, the blond pop star who had once adorned every teenager's bedroom wall. Childhood fantasy was fast becoming reality. His modest life in Warrington was well and truly relegated to the past. Once asked if he missed his home town he quipped, 'Yeah I try to miss it every time I go past on the motorway.' Many of those left behind remain far from amused by the attitude of their town's most famous export.

By the beginning of the next year he was ready to air a new TV show, TFI Friday. This raucous chat and music based show, though packed with star guests, would prove to be another vehicle for Evans' considerable talents. He secured a £15 million deal with Channel Four to produce and present the show.

At the height of his career in 1997, Evans unexpectedly resigned from his dream job at Radio One, complaining that Matthew Bannister would not give him adequate time off to pursue his TV work. In December of that year, Evans pulled his most ambitious coup to date when he bought Virgin Radio. The experience at Radio One convinced him of the need to be in complete control. He used his business savvy and vast media influence to convince a consortium to invest £85 million in a take-over bid for Virgin Radio, which would make Evans the major shareholder. Barbara Manfrey, a corporate financier for Apax Partners, the investment group who played a major part in the take-over, says candidly of Evans, 'he knows exactly what he's doing...he has an encyclopaedic knowledge of radio and TV.' A measure of Evans' ambition was the fact that he had slipped in ahead of Capital Radio, London's largest commercial station, who had been forced to delay their purchase of Virgin. Certainly, Richard Branson, the former owner, who still has a stake in the station's fortune, was not disheartened by this, enthusing, 'The maverick in me prefers the idea of Chris Evans to Capital Radio - the station will be in good hands.'

In this heady atmosphere of public success, private happiness was still as distant as ever. Evans has often been described as a control freak - always desperate for praise and attention, he seems to need constant sycophantic attention. When Grundy first went to visit the DJ in London, he was not surprised to find him accompanied by 'an entourage of five, six, seven people - the kind who laugh at him and stroke his ego.' This would appear to be evidence of a continued sense of insecurity. Tim Grundy continues, '...In reality you have a fundamentally unhappy man, who has been frighteningly single-minded in his determination to succeed; who has used and abused those around him; and hasn't finished in his endless quest for power and glory.' One of Grundy's most biting criticisms concerns Evans's tendency to use people: 'There are so many of his old friends, people I would have called real friends who, after he found success, just wanted to contact him and say well done, or how's it going, or shall we meet up and have a meal; but he cut them all off if they couldn't be of use to him. Such descriptions belie the witty and (sometimes) loveable screen persona.

In recent months, it appears that, even on a professional level, Evans is experiencing burn-out. His breakfast show on Virgin has, reportedly, been losing listeners at an alarming rate, and a televised version of the same show has been slated by the public and critics alike. Could it be that the erratic persona that has in turn offended colleagues and delighted audiences, has finally lost its appeal? Perhaps; yet, Evans remains as high-profile and powerful as ever. Throughout his brief career, his immense enthusiasm and resourcefulness has allowed him to reach his own sky-high expectations. In return for his industry and unfaltering desire to succeed, he has received wealth and fame. This may not prove the key to happiness; yet fame and happiness are two very different concepts.

FRANK SINATRA
1915 - 1998

By 1952, the skinny teen sensation from Hoboken was professionally dead. His song style was no longer fashionable, tantrums and unadulterated arrogance had made him a film studio pariah, even his booking agents dropped him. As Sinatra's professional life crumbled, a passionate and controversial affair with screen star Ava Gardner ended a habitually unfaithful marriage to his childhood sweetheart. With so many burnt bridges behind him, Sinatra looked like another victim of fame. Yet, less than a year later he had crawled out of the trough and was gaining chart and film success once again.

Fortune favours the brave and Sinatra's guts, self belief and an uncanny ability to manipulate people and situations enabled him to make one of the greatest comebacks in entertainment history. He had the instincts of a terrier: grab something and never let go. A cocky Italian 'wise guy', he may have been, but Sinatra had a truly unique singing style which remains fresh to this day. Much has been written about his lifestyle, his temper, womanising, shady associations and politics. What remains a constant is that voice. Whereas singers like Bing Crosby sang with a studied gracefulness, Sinatra, influenced by African-American vocals, emphasised emotion rather than perfection. This emphasis has become the norm in modern popular music.

Francis Albert Sinatra was born on 12 December 1915 in his parents tenement apartment in Hoboken, New Jersey. Looking across the Hudson River to Manhattan, it had always been a stop off for newly arrived immigrants and by 1924, Italians made up the largest minority group. Hoboken, once a retreat for the rich, became a heaving industrial town. Sinatra's difficult breech birth seemed to portend a difficult future. With a punctured ear drum and facial scars from the use of forceps, the doctor left Sinatra for dead to save his mother. It was only his grandmother putting him under cold water which revived him. Sinatra's mother would never bear another child and Sinatra wore his scars as a symbol of his first struggle.

Sinatra grew up as an only child amongst a community of large families. His Sicilian father, Martin Sinatra, had fought in the ring as Marty O'Brian, and had dabbled in bootlegging during the prohibition, an activity which resulted in Marty O'Brian's Bar. Quiet and hard working, he was dominated by his wife.

In a male dominated community, it was Sinatra's energetic mother, Dolly who guided her family. A feminist before her time, it was through her endeavours that the family went from tenement to four bedroom house. As a midwife who performed abortions during a period when such practices were prohibited, she displayed a compassionate pragmatism, 'I know what I am doing, God knows what I'm doing'. This self assurance in the face of opposition left the most indelible mark on Sinatra's character. When he said in later life, 'I am what I am and I'm not asking myself any questions...,' his mother's influence is clearly audible.

He also inherited Dolly's habit of buying influence. As a Ward Healer, she secured Frank's first important breaks. A Ward Healer was essentially a political boss, a fixer who took care of neighbours' problems in exchange for votes. A trading permit could be obtained by promising loyalty on election day. The election winners and their supporters could expect jobs and millions in kick-backs. Dolly effectively scratched backs to get her family out of poverty: Martin became a fireman, eventually rising to the rank of Captain despite his illiteracy. The young Sinatra's loneliness and distance from his mother were compensated by clothes, gifts and money. Nicknamed Slacksie O'Brian on account of innumerable suits and trousers, he learnt the art of buying his friendship very quickly from his wheeling dealing mother. In later life Sinatra gained the reputation for lavishing extravagant gifts on his cronies.

Sinatra was lazy and lacked concentration, leaving school at fifteen. Distraught at his academic failure, Dolly managed to secure him work but his cocky attitude always got him the sack. Job followed job, each one going the same way - resignation or sacking; meanwhile, Sinatra was considering a singing career, an occupation which went against the grain of his hard working immigrant parents.

Sinatra was not a natural singer and it is a measure of his unerring self-discipline that he transformed a high, reedy voice into one of the most distinctive instruments in the business. By the time he was seventeen he was performing for free with local bands at functions and school dances; his parents could not ignore what seemed to be his first serious passion. True to form, Dolly lent him S65 to buy a portable PA system and the latest sheet music arrangements. With this important bargaining chip Sinatra brought together semi-professionals for gigs, on the condition that he sang. After two years of constant singing, Sinatra had gained a reputation and began a regular stint at the local Union Club.

Sinatra's first real break came in September 1930 when he teamed up with the Hoboken singing group The Three Flashes to perform on Major Bowes And His Amateur Hour, broadcast live on NBC Radio. Rumour has it that Dolly may have influenced the Hoboken based group to take her son on. What is certain is that the group, now called The Hoboken Four, were an instant success and would spend 1935 touring the country with Major Bowes' cabaret. Sinatra had now replaced the lead singer, but after months of (often physical) abuse from the other group members, he decided to go solo. Clearly jealous of Sinatra's burgeoning success, their treatment of him gives some credence to the rumours of Dolly's influence in securing her son's job. In 1938 Sinatra became a singing waiter at The Rustic Cabin, a New Jersey restaurant with a live link to the New York radio station WNEW. After her son failed his first audition, Dolly contacted the New Jersey Musicians Union boss, to ensure that his second audition would be successful.

Despite the glaring fact that his mother had secured the job, Sinatra was brimming with confidence and boasting that he was a talent for the future, although fellow musicians ridiculed his grandiose claims. In February 1939 Sinatra married his teenage sweet-heart Nancy Barbato, a local girl who was willing to support Sinatra's aspirations. Yet with a string of affairs behind him, it was clear that the brash young singer's marriage to the devoted home-maker was doomed from the start.

The singing lessons and nightly sets at The Rustic Cabin were honing Sinatra's voice into an original style, removed from the popular Bing Crosby approach and gaining recognition from both audiences and professionals. One such professional and a WNEW listener was the band leader Harry James. Big Bands dominated the airwaves and provided the backdrop for lovers and the frenetic 'Jitterbug' tunes which set auditoriums alight. Singers were a poor cousin to the horn players of the day and could expect to sing only a couple of chorus lines. When Harry James went to check out the singing-waiter, he was simply looking for a chorus singer. After hiring him, however, it soon became clear to James that Sinatra had an unusual talent for imbuing lyrics with emotion. As James recounted in 1971, 'When Frank joined the band he was always thinking of the lyrics. The melody was secondary. If it was a delicate or pretty word, he would try to phrase it with a prettier, softer type of voice.'

Recognising a niche in the market for vocals, all ten of James' arrangements between July and November 1939 were centred around Sinatra's singing and a new trend began. However, the relatively unknown band was still only just scraping a living. Tommy Dorsey's band, the most successful and talented of the era, was also feeling the pinch from increasing competition. In search of a new angle in the battle for airplay and ticket sales, he looked to the New Jersey crooner. Sinatra's unyielding ambition, tempered by the need to provide for Nancy, who was pregnant with Nancy Jnr., led him to join Dorsey and he parted from Harry James on amiable terms.

Sinatra referred to his time with Dorsey (1939-1942) as his greatest learning period. Although many of the musicians took a dislike to his temerity, Sinatra took full advantage of learning from some of the best men in the business. Dorsey began concentrating on vocals rather than instrumental pieces and in May 1940 the transition paid off when 'I'll Never Smile Again' was a number one hit for twelve weeks. The era of the Pop Star had arrived.

The following May Billboard Magazine named the 25 year-old as top male singer. By the end of the year he had beaten Bing Crosby, his personal bench mark, as most popular singer. Sinatra's ambition told him to go solo but Dorsey refused to let his best asset go. There were whispers that Sinatra's boss Hank Sanicola hired some New Jersey toughs to extricate Sinatra from Dorsey's contract. Tommy Dorsey, himself a tough businessman, is said to have sworn and cursed as he signed away the papers. Sinatra would persistently deny these rumours.

One of the biggest myths in popular culture is that Elvis Presley was the first singing sex symbol. Years earlier, teenage girls were screaming and fainting at Sinatra concerts. Sinatra had mastered the hesitant word or fleeting glance to make every member of the audience feel he was singing to them. Sinatra's first solo appearance in Manhattan in December 1942 was greeted with a cacophony of screams: Sinatramania was born. His fans were predominantly 13 or 14 year-olds, (called 'Bobby Soxers') too young for real boyfriends. With men at war, Sinatra became a female focus. One journalist dubbed him 'Swoonatra' after the epidemic of fainting fans and by 1943 he had two thousand fan clubs. A year later the Sinatra frenzy had reached a new pitch when fans, unable to get into a performance, rioted . In 1943, Bill Evans, Sinatra's new publicist, realised that the 27 year old husband and father needed to attract an older and less fickle audience. The shift proved successful and at his first 'serious' performance he managed to impress sceptical musicians and journalists with his interpretative singing style and professionalism.

Sinatra's success lay in his adaptability. He managed to make the transition to recording artist when live performance dominated. He knew his market and could pick a good song. A string of hits between 1943 and 1944 led him to record his first album. The Voice in 1945, the first album to reach number one in the new Billboard charts and the first of 75 hit albums spanning six decades. For many, Sinatra symbolises American music of the 1940s.

During the last year with the Dorsey band, Sinatra's film career began when he appeared in two movies. The 1941 musical Las Vegas Nights was followed by Ship Ahoy and Sinatra, ever the opportunist, saw a vehicle for further personal success. In 1944, impressed by Sinatra's rendition of 'Ol' Man River,' Louis B Meyer, the head of MGM Films signed the singer for a $1.5 million five year contract. Frank Sinatra was now the highest paid entertainer in the world and the family, now including Francis Junior, moved to Hollywood. In the same year Sinatra appeared with Gene Kelly in Anchors Aweigh, an instant success. Sinatra had not only wrested the crown from Bing Crosby as the world's favourite crooner but was fast entering the silver screen stratosphere.

Sinatra's move to Los Angeles almost destroyed his career. A city which scandalised conservative America, it was the worst place for a man of Sinatra's libido and ego. In New York it had been relatively easy for Evans to cover up the singer's various sexual indiscretions, but under the claustrophobic glare of Hollywood's media, every vice became common knowledge. It was no longer the case of 'what Nancy doesn't know won't hurt her'. Affairs with the likes of Lana Turner became part of the public preserve.

In the late 1940s and early 1950s, Sinatra's private life was overtaking his career and he became a prime target for the increasingly vitriolic and powerful gossip columns. His popularity suffered as the image of clean living family man turned into that of philandering rat. A naturally inflated ego allied to wealth and fame resulted in increasingly public tantrums which only increased column inches.

Rather than pander to the press, Sinatra met them head on. Verbal and written threats led to a physical attack on the particularly venomous columnist Lee Mortimer, resulting in court action and a $9,000 fine. Today, attacking photographers seems de rigueur for successful stars; forty years ago it confirmed to many that Sinatra was just an Italian low-life.

As a child in a tough neighbourhood, whose father had inhabited the underworld peripheries, Sinatra had always been impressed by hoodlums. With money and fame he was now able to associate with the Mafia, an association which did nothing for his public image. His naive visit to the Chicago boss Lucky Luciano in Havana resulted in the right-wing columnist Robert Ruark reporting on the Sinatra-Mafia connection. A rumour was born and the FBI began investigating these connections. Sinatra was already being investigated by the Bureau for accusations of communist sympathies, stemming from his prominence in a campaign promoting racial and religious tolerance. He starred in the critically acclaimed 1944 anti-racist short film The House I Live In. Sinatra, a lifelong Democrat, was a very vocal anti racist and although the communist allegation was clearly unsubstantiated, it did not help his reputation.

If success continues, bad personal press can be endured, however in 1948 he appeared in two film flops, The Miracle of the Bells and The Kissing Bandit. In 1949 Sinatra's career and private life spiralled downwards. Axed from MGM, following a remark concerning Louis B Meyer's sex life, he was listed as fifth most popular singer, the first time he was out of the top three since the late 1930s. Big Bands were out and Sinatra no longer fitted the taste for short Juke-Box length songs. His very public affair with the screen goddess, Ava Gardner, resulted in his separation with Nancy and his three children in 1948, causing public outrage. In 1950 Bill Evans predicted Sinatra's downfall after being sacked for not supporting this relationship: 'Frank is through. A year from now you won't hear anything about him. He'll be dead professionally...The public knows about the trouble about

Nancy now, and the other dames, and it doesn't like him anymore'.

The prediction came true. In 1951, following his divorce from Nancy, and marriage to Ava Gardner he appeared in two flops including Meet Danny Wilson, a film about a nasty night club singer which seemed to caricature his own life. An on-set tantrum in that film blew his chances of future work. In 1952, with no offers of film work, Sinatra's contract with Columbia Records was not renewed.

When asked in 1955, what caused his downfall, Sinatra replied, 'Me, I did it. I'm my own worst enemy.' For someone of Sinatra's arrogance, this was a tremendous admission, showing how hard his fall from public grace had been. His marriage to Ava Gardner, only added to these dark days. The tempestuous pair enjoyed the wild life, but as her career waxed, his waned, a pressure adding to an already turbulent relationship. With a failed suicide attempt in 1951, he had hit the bottom, succumbing to increasingly irrational mood swings.

Sinatra said in later life, 'Don't despair, you have to scrape the bottom to appreciate life and start living again'. Surviving his most testing time, Sinatra managed one of the greatest comebacks in entertainment history. Ironically, the abrasive attitude which had caused his downfall, along with an instinct for self-preservation, helped him back to the top.

In 1952, Sinatra heard that Columbia Pictures were making a film of the best seller From Here to Eternity. The book was centred around soldiers in Pearl Harbour at the time of the Japanese attack. Sinatra knew he was perfect for the part of Maggio, a skinny, noisy Italian who dies at the end of the film: 'I knew Maggio, I went to High School with him in Hoboken.' Trusting his gut feeling and with the help of Ava's influence, the producer Harry Cohn, after continuous harassment, gave him a screen test. Despite a good test, first choice went to Eli Wallach. However, when Wallach turned down the part, it went to Sinatra: the studio pariah was back in business.

The film, starring Montgomery Clift, Deborah Kerr and Burt Lancaster was one of the most successful films of 1953. Perhaps the brash, irritating part came easy to Sinatra but in 1954 he received an Oscar for best supporting actor. He had turned a comer. In 1953 his emotionally draining marriage to Ava Gardner ended and he concentrated on his career.

A man who had been earning a million a couple of years before, had accepted the Maggio part for $8,000. In 1953, without a record contract, Sinatra secured a one year deal with the successful independent label, Capitol Records on the proviso that he would pay studio costs: He was beginning again from scratch.

The Capitol years (1954-1957) are an era of unbridled creativity with seven out of ten albums reaching the top ten. Classic albums such as In The Wee Small Hours (1955) and Songs For Swinging Lovers (1956) are regarded as the first real concept albums and have stood the test of time. The depth of feeling in Sinatra's voice is the mark of a man who stared into the abyss and came back.

Sinatra had an effortlessly relaxed sound unlike the studied singing technique of Crosby. It was a thoroughly modern style which set the standard for pop singers today. This was his 'Swinging' period, all coolness and charm. It is an attitude which still impresses musicians. As U2's Bono explained, when presenting Sinatra with a Legend award at the 1994 Grammy Awards: 'Rock 'n Roll people love Frank Sinatra because Frank Sinatra has got what we want...swagger and attitude'.

Sinatra was the biggest selling album artist between 1955-1959 and consolidated his acting reputation with his Oscar nominated portrayal of the heroin addicted gambler in the controversial The Man with the Golden Arm (1955). His reversal in fortune was confirmed by his appearance on the front cover of Time as the richest entertainer ever. The decade ended with the hit album Come Dance With Me which won a Grammy Award. At the age of forty, Sinatra could do no wrong.

The music industry is littered with musicians who have suffered at the hands business sharks. Sinatra is one of the few exceptions. Back in the '40s he had set up his own music publishing company Sinatra Songs, having learnt from Dorsey the art of picking popular tunes. In 1960 he set up his Reprise label of which the first five releases in 1961, including a Sinatra album, were successful. He was in the unusual position of competing with himself, as Capitol were also releasing his albums. By 1963 Reprise was an extremely successful label and Sinatra sold two thirds of it to Warner Brothers.

Sinatra's personal life was also making waves in this period. The early 1960s belonged to 'The Rat Pack', the now legendary group of friends who cruised and boozed around the Las Vegas' casinos and clubs. Sinatra held court to Dean Martin, Sammy Davis Jnr., Peter Lawford (JFK's brother-in law) and comic Joey Bishop. Their style, antics and Rat Pack films such as Ocean's Eleven (1960), culturally define a small but significant part of American history.

The Rat Pack's support for John F. Kennedy's presidential campaign ushered in the high profile use of show business for political gain. However, Sinatra's support for JFK coincided with his Mafia connections. It is surprising that Sinatra couldn't recognise such conflicting relationships. Perhaps he saw himself as a power broker, taking his cue from Dolly's Ward Healing days. The mob boss Sam Giancana, frustrated by continued FBI surveillance, saw Sinatra as a key to political influence. However, JFK, concerned by FBI reports about Sinatra's Mafia contacts and notorious lifestyle, cut off relations from a genuinely hurt Sinatra. Sam Giancana, realising that Sinatra was of little use also retreated. In a bizarre twist, Frank starred in the 1962 film classic The Manchurian Candidate, about the assassination of a president. The next year JFK was assassinated in Dallas. By the mid 1960s Sinatra had already become a living legend. A marriage to Mia Farrow in 1966, a string of high profile relationships (including links to Jackie Onassis), his jet-set lifestyle and speculation about his Mafia links kept Sinatra in the public eye. Although it seems his Mob fascination fizzled out during the following years, his casino share-holdings, ensured continued Mafia connections throughout the 1960s-70s. In 1970 he was subpoenaed to testify under oath about these connections but still denied any knowledge.

In 1971, after a record seventy four hit albums, he temporarily retired as a recording artist. A maturing Sinatra, eager to project a more respectable image, concentrated on live charity concerts. In his 1975 world tour, Sinatra made an astounding 140 performances in only 150 days, entertaining more than half a million fans. His years as a concert performer were immortalized by the 1979 classic New York, New York.

A fourth marriage to Barbara Marx in 1976 tamed the playboy and in the 1980s Sinatra was like an elder statesman performing to presidents and dignitaries. He received America's highest civilian award, The Presidential Medal of Freedom in 1985. Yet in the 1990s a new generation of listeners were becoming drawn to the Sinatra phenomenon. His 75th birthday in 1990 was marked by a national tour and in 1996 he won yet another Grammy award for his album Duets II a collaborative work with other stars.

When Sinatra died of a heart attack on May 15 1998 it was a tragic end to an era. He defined what it meant to be an entertainer, setting trends and manipulating the Zeitgeist of successive decades. In the 1940s he created the cult of the pop star. His laid back vocals influenced a legion of imitators and set the standards by which successive pop artists sing. Sinatra was the master of emotion, imbuing lyrics with subtle meaning that can be universally understood. Like many performers he was lonely. Distanced from a strong mother and having a bad history with women, his inner turmoil enriched his powers of expression. Sinatra summed it up by saying, 'Being an 18 karat manic depressive and having lived a life of violent emotional contradictions, I have an over acute capacity for sadness as well as elation. I know what the cat who wrote the song is saying. I've been there and back...'

Sinatra had unprecedented success in one of the toughest industries. No other musician has come close to having the same amount of album hits over the last fifty years. He won critical acclaim for his singing and acting; it is difficult to think of modem equivalent whose talent could justify such a dual career. Yet it could have been very different; by 1951, Sinatra was written off. An innate arrogance, obnoxious temper and womanising destroyed the years of hard work and determination which had made him a star. But it was these very qualities, plus self belief and an instinct for self preservation, which turned around his self inflicted failure into extraordinary success. He never bowed to public or media opinion, trusting only his talent. The 1969 hit, 'My Way' is Sinatra's epitaph: he faced failure and overcame it despite the odds. Unlike Buddy Holly or Elvis Presley, he became a legend precisely because he lived on.

TONY BLAIR
1953 - PRESENT DAY

On the First of May 1997, Britain voted to place the Labour Party into government. Their leader, Tony Blair, at forty-three, became the youngest Prime Minister since Lord Liverpool entered 10 Downing Street, 185 years earlier. This crowning achievement came surprisingly swiftly for Blair. Even his most optimistic estimates must have time-tabled the promotion years into his political future. A decade earlier, he had wandered in the political wilderness, scouring the constituencies for a vacant seat. Now as the architect of New Labour, he carries the hopes of an expectant British nation.

Anthony Charles Lynton Blair was bomb on 6 May 1953 in Edinburgh, Scotland. He was the second of Leo and Hazel Blair's three children. The family moved to Australia when he was eighteen months old, following his father's acceptance of a job as lecturer at the University of Adelaide.

Leo Blair hailed from working-class roots but his academic aspirations yielded a comfortable middle-class lifestyle. In 1958, while he completed his work in Adelaide, the rest of the family flew back to Britain and settled in Durham. After a six month separation, he rejoined them after attaining the post of lecturer at Durham University. The academic was clearly drifting away from his humble background; a trend made conspicuous by his membership of the Conservative Party. A desire to further his career and enter politics was equally manifest when he became chairman of the local Conservative Association in 1964. This was to be just the start. His real ambition was to become Prime Minister.

At this point, all was rosy in the Blair household. Tony Blair was a bright, inquisitive child, known for a love of performing before an audience. The prosperous family could afford to send him and his older brother to Choristers School, where they enjoyed the benefits of a private education. In general, he seems to have enjoyed a cheerful childhood. In 1994, he reflected back to this period, revealing in an interview on Channel Four News: 'We had a perfectly good, average, middle-class standard of living.' Yet midway through this period of harmony, an unforeseen occurrence would turn the household upside down.

In 1964, Leo Blair suffered a serious stroke which ended both his lecturing career and political aspirations, leaving him unable to speak. It was a defining moment for the family; Tony later termed it 'one of the formative events of my life.' It also rested a considerable burden on his shoulders: 'After his illness my father transferred his ambitions onto his kids. It imposed a certain discipline. I felt I couldn't let him down.' From this sense of duty to his father's ambition, he was infused with the desire, perhaps the compulsion, to succeed.

Blair was forced to view the world in a different light. He had to watch as his father's hard work and aspirations faded. But his father's conservative values and his political work in Durham, were, no doubt, major influences. Similarly, a sense of work-ethic and dedication would never leave him.

Leo Blair naturally wanted the best for his children, and for this reason his son was enrolled at Fettes Boarding School. To begin with, Tony was unimpressed with the harsh regime. The institutionalised bullying inherent in the 'fagging' system, where the younger boys performed the role of servants to the older boys, did little to alleviate his distaste. The negative aspects of his new environment affected him to such an extent that on a number of occasions he ran away from the school. Gradually he absorbed himself in the system and became a promising pupil, excelling in sports and becoming known as a budding actor. Yet, during his later years he became increasingly disenchanted. He was popular but often exhibited an argumentative and rebellious streak. His behaviour was not simply wayward or disruptive, and he has been described as an 'intellectual rebel'. As former tutor, David Kennedy, explains: 'Some boys are rebellious because they are stupid. Tony was rebellious because he wanted to question all the values we held to.' Nevertheless, in his final year, at the age of seventeen, Blair was given six lashes of the cane by a house master who branded him 'the most difficult boy I ever had to deal with.' When Blair reflected back to his time at Fettes it was with mixed feelings. In 1991, he explained that although the public school system allowed him to gain relatively good exam results, he did not feel that it furnished him with other essential qualities: 'The problem with the public school system is that you end up being a highly competent sitter of exams, but you haven't necessarily got much confidence.'

Blair moved on to Oxford University to read Law. During these years he began to think seriously about his future. In his years at Oxford, Blair was active in all circles. He was content to follow the usual student lifestyle, enjoying trips to pubs and theatres, and even becoming the singer of a student rock band - 'The Ugly Rumours'. Yet, he was equally happy to spend considerable time enjoying the solitude of the library and participating in late night discussions on philosophy and religion with a group of mature students. He was obviously open to new people and ideas; the ability to relate to all types of people would prove crucial to his later political appeal.

At Oxford, Blair was strongly influenced by an Australian mature student, Peter Thompson, and the writings of John MacMurray, a Scottish philosopher. He once described Thompson as 'the person who most influenced me.' A mature student of philosophy, Thompson used to invite other students around to his flat to take part in informal chats, discussing religion, philosophy and politics. Key to the discussions were the ideas of John MacMurray, notably his preoccupation with how to balance individual interest with the good of society as a whole. MacMurray's ideas fed into Blair's own Christian thinking, giving it a political and practical edge. In his second year at Oxford, Blair was confirmed into the Church of England. Years later, his religious convictions would form the foundation of his political creed of 'social moralism'.

Blair graduated in 1975. Two weeks later his mother died of cancer. This was another crushing blow, but by all accounts he was able to remain composed enough to take care of his distraught father and younger sister. Hazel Blair's death forced her son to face some harsh realities and further strengthened his resolve to make a difference. He spoke candidly about the loss: 'As well as your own grief for the person your own mortality comes home to you. And you suddenly realise - which often you don't do as a young person - that life is finite, so if you want things done you better get a move on.'

Blair certainly did 'get a move on'. In the same year he joined the Labour Party; the following year he successfully applied for a scholarship to train as a lawyer. His ability to project a charismatic and intelligent persona was central to his acceptance at the London offices of Alexander Irvine QC. Irvine had already taken on one of the most outstanding prospects in the country, one Cherie Booth. Instead of becoming rivals, Blair and Booth's relationship blossomed. In 1976, Blair was called to the Bar, where he began to work full time for Irvine as a barrister. Irvine said of Blair: 'He was absolutely excellent. I have no doubt that he would he become a QC.' A promising career in Law was clearly beckoning, but Blair's increasing involvement with his local branch of the Labour Party was pulling him in another direction. He had been considering a political career for some time.

In 1980, Tony and Cherie were married in Oxford. The newlyweds moved to London, where Blair prepared to turn political ambition into political power. He became a rigorous, and increasingly well-known, local activist. The Labour Party at this time was in turmoil. Struggling against internal divisions, as well as a powerful Conservative Government, they were in desperate need of a leader who could bring unity. In future years Blair would fulfil this need, but he had a long way to climb before he reached that stage.

Charles Falconer, who knew Blair well at this point, remarked in regard to his friend's eventual succession to the leadership: 'It's quite surprising. But he has got a sort of determined, self-disciplined, slightly obsessive quality, which makes him the sort of person who will become leader of the Labour Party.'

Blair experienced his first political battle when he stood as the Labour candidate for the safe Conservative seat of Beaconsfield, in a 1982 by-election. He received only ten percent of the vote, trailing home in a disappointing third place. He was distressed but not discouraged. Undeterred, he continued to make friends and influence people, always leaving a positive impression in his wake.

Known for his detailed research and preparation, Blair stood out as a confident media performer. His peers could not but be impressed. Mike Gapes, the researcher who briefed Blair on party policy, recalled: 'I don't remember any other by-election candidates in the early eighties asking for a briefing. He was serious and thorough. He wanted to know what the line was. He was keen, quite diffident, but very sharp. He asked all the right questions.' Blair was always extremely conscious of the need to convey the right media image: relaxed, confident and ready for any question. In politics, a childhood interest in acting is seldom wasted.

The following year, Blair was once again desperately seeking a constituency. His prospects looked bleak; the majority of the London seats were already taken. With nothing to lose, he began to search further a-field. As he scoured the country for an opportunity, he discovered that the constituency of Sedgefield (in the north of England) had yet to nominate a candidate. He needed no further encouragement. Blair set about selling himself to the local party members using his penchant for direct personal canvassing. The diffident character had to summon up all his courage; Blair, carrying the weight of his father's ambition, was determined to make the most of the opportunity. If he failed it would not be for want of trying. Paul Trippet, one of the committee members Blair needed to win-over, recalled the situation: 'We were less than a month away from an election, he didn't have a nomination, he was going to a branch that didn't have an inclination to nominate anybody particularly, going to a stranger's house to meet some people, and he just thought, "What am I doing here?" He sat there for a minute or two, and then thought, "I've come all this way, I might as well go in."'

The Shadow Home Secretary at this time was Roy Hattersley. He vividly recalls being woken by an assistant and informed: 'Young Blair's done this extraordinary thing. He hadn't been short-listed, and he's gone around and knocked on all the doors. And he's got it.' At this point, Hattersley saw the rich potential in 'young Blair'. His belief was fully vindicated as Blair went on to win the seat in the 1983 general election with a majority of over eight thousand votes. But Blair's personal jubilation at becoming an MP was tempered by the dismal failure of his party. Buoyed by victory in the Falklands War, Margaret Thatcher and the Tory Party swept back into power. With just twenty-eight percent of the national vote, the Labour Party were, once again, very much in second place.

At thirty, Blair was the youngest Labour MP in the Commons. In the forthcoming years he progressed steadily within the party, keeping his views close to those of the leader, Michael Foot. His loyalty did not go unnoticed with the leadership. Blair soon found himself touted as a bright prospect for the future. In 1984, he was given the position of Assistant Treasury Spokesman. Blair worked his way seamlessly through the ranks, treading carefully among delicate egos. In 1987, under the leadership of Neil Kinnock, he was promoted to Deputy Spokesman on Trade and Industry.

After another general election defeat, Kinnock pushed for radical change within the party. A new group of modernisers, including Blair, attempted to target 'middle England' by reviewing party policy on unilateral disarmament, links with the trade unions and Europe. Their dream was a strong power base outside the old class politics. It was a vision partly borne out of frustration and many traditional Labour members viewed the change of direction as a betrayal of socialism. Nevertheless, the group took it upon themselves to 're-brand' the party.

Intelligent, articulate and ambitious, Blair had joined the small clique of Labour hopefuls being groomed for the top. This elite group also included Gordon Brown, who, in 1987, became deputy to the Shadow Chancellor (and future leader) John Smith. In particular, Blair and Brown were given considerable responsibility early on in their political careers. Both continued to justify the faith invested in them. The relationship between Blair and Brown was close, but an underlying rivalry was somewhat inevitable. Only one of them could realistically become leader, and they both knew it. In future years, this central relationship would become the focus of much media attention. Despite numerous denials to the contrary, many commentators insist that the rivalry lives on.

In 1992, Blair made a rare error, procrastinating over whether or not to run for the deputy leadership. He had his sights firmly set on the top job but was unsure about how to achieve it. A year later, he took another step forward, becoming Shadow Home Secretary. With the importance of image always to the forefront of his thinking, he expanded his close team of advisors to ensure the media was as favourable as possible. He was by now a very prominent politician, admired by supporters and respected by rivals.

On May 2, 1994, Blair received momentous news. The Labour leader, John Smith, had died of a heart attack. Its personal and political implications for Blair were profound. Once again, tragedy was a spur to ambition. The path to the leadership was clear. Blair remembered his hesitation in the 1992 deputy leadership contest. Never one to repeat a mistake, he put himself forward in the knowledge that he was the clear favourite. The leadership election would have certainly been a more interesting battle if Brown had contested it. However, knowing he was the less telegenic of the two, Brown decided to support his friend. He knew his place in a future Labour cabinet was secure. It was, thus, no great surprise when, on 21 July 1994, Blair was declared leader of the Labour Party. It later transpired that he had even been John Smith's preferred choice as his eventual successor. Yet, Blair's accession had come much quicker than expected, and his new position must have been daunting.

In the following years, Blair stepped up the modernisation of the party. A new media friendly approach, incorporating catchy (if somewhat superficial) sound-bites, became the hall-mark of his leadership. He was also busy redefining socialism: 'It stands for co-operation, not confrontation... It stands for equality not because it wants people to be the same but because only through equality in our economic circumstances can our individuality develop properly.' For some traditional Labour supporters, the party was moving too far, too fast, from its old values, in the search for middle class votes. In August 1995, Roy Hattersley, voiced the grassroots concern, arguing that Blair had 'begun to overlook the needs of the disadvantaged and the dispossessed.' Yet, the new approach was working, and the Labour laddie was not for turning.

Blair struck a nerve by deciding to send his son to a selective school, rather than to his local comprehensive. Some party members felt that, as leader, he should have set an example rather than going against the heart of Labour education policy. Murmurs of discontent were also caused by Blair's plans to court the business world, while distancing himself from the now uncomfortable ties with the trade unions. This move was made crystal clear when Blair decided to rewrite Clause IV of the Labour Party constitution. The clause, untouched since 1917, stressed the importance of socialist values and union power. In 1995, Blair's bold move was supported by a majority of conference delegates. The leader had been willing to put his reputation at stake in the cause of reform.

With the considerable assistance of arch Labour spin-doctor, Peter Mandelson, Blair was able to cash-in on the issue of Tory sleaze, and the public's growing aversion to the government. Conservative attempts to vilify Blair with their notorious 'demon eyes' poster, or ridicule him as 'Tony the Phoney', were less successful. In the 1997 general election, Blair easily turned the tide to steer a revitalised New Labour Party to victory. His campaign had been characterised by a unity and discipline conspicuously absent from recent Labour failures. Despite a careful approach and fairly modest proposals, Labour's campaign song - 'Things can only get better' - struck a clear chord with the voters. At the centre of it all was the winning smile of Tony Blair. His appeal to all sectors of society was obvious. His charm offensive before the image-obsessed and sound bite friendly media was relentless. But was there more to the new Prime Minister than a carefully crafted media image?

Four months after the election, Princess Diana was killed in a car crash. Blair's resulting tribute to the 'people's princess' again struck a chord with a public in mourning. In fact, the much-repeated phrase was coined by his able press secretary, Alastair Campbell. Another triumph for public relations, or a sincere Prime Minister in tune with his nation? The phrase spread - Blair became 'the people's Prime Minister.' The tabloids reported on glitzy celebrity parties Blair held at No. 10, to thank his supporters. Blair was at the centre of the much vaunted media invention known as 'Cool Britannia'. He was at the summit of 'New Britain'. Meanwhile, critics, both inside and outside the Labour party, began to complain of a pandering to popular culture, of the triumph of style over content. Yet, the strenuous talks concerning the troubles in Northern Ireland, which resulted in the signing of the Good Friday Peace Agreement, revealed the Prime Minister to be a persuasive and persistent negotiator. Outside the media circus, he sought to implement the modest pledges he had promised to the voters. Perhaps it is too simplistic (and too early) to dismiss Blair as a superficial politician bringing merely cosmetic change.

The cruel curtailment of his father's ambition was the decisive step in Blair's progress to the top. He has fought his way into government through a combination of charm, control and determination. Due to his ability to appeal to voters of all social backgrounds, he has made a sudden and decisive impact on British politics. If he can weather the storms that lie ahead, and convert the positive rhetoric into lasting change, Tony Blair may well prove all his critics wrong.

IMRAN KHAN
1952 - PRESENT DAY

When athletes retire, it is usually to run pubs, commentate on matches or make the move into pantomime or television. It can honestly be said that only one sportsman has quit at the very peak of his career to run a cancer hospital for the poverty stricken inhabitants of his hometown or entered the cut-throat and often corrupt world of Asian politics. He is Imran Khan, Pakistan's most famous cricketer and, without doubt, the country's most recognisable personality.

As a player, his all-round ability was legendary. He was as adept with the bat as he was with the ball; his vicious 'inswingers' and notorious 'bouncers' devastated teams the world over from England to Australia. Outside the sporting arena, his projects have ranged from writing books and newspaper articles to the establishment of the Shaukat Khanum Memorial Cancer Hospital. His mystic Hollywoodesque good looks have been much commented on; model and television presenter Marie Helvin stated that, 'no man looks as devastating as Imran... everyone falls for him.' In Britain, he has been viewed as a dashing cricketer and a gifted humanitarian; in Pakistan, he has been held in almost Godlike reverence.

Born on 25 November 1952, in Lahore, Pakistan, Imran Khan was the only son (though he had four sisters) of Ikramullah Niazi and Shaukat Khan. Imran, himself, described his upbringing as both 'privileged and cosseted.' Ikramullah, his father, was a brilliant engineer who, after gaining a postgraduate degree from Imperial College, London, had joined the Government service. His mother's family was already moneyed and comfortable. Imran's background was solidly upper middle class and, in comparison with the horrendous poverty that affected their fellow countrymen, his family were positively affluent.

The school he attended, Aitchison College, in Lahore, was the equivalent of England's Eton or Harrow. It was here and on the lush playing fields of the exclusive Gymkhana Club that his passion for cricket was born. A passion that would soon become an obsession. Linder the watchful eyes of two of Pakistan's finest cricketers Javed Burki and Majid Khan, who also happened to be Imran's cousins, the young lad's game quickly improved yet was still far from outstanding.

In 1968, at the age of sixteen, he made his first class debut for his home team, Lahore. Imran's performance was not overly auspicious; two wickets and thirty-two runs. He could only improve and with typical tenacity he did just that. During the 1970-71 season, he was the second highest wicket taker in Pakistani domestic cricket and in 1971, at the tender age of nineteen, he had impressed the selectors enough to pick him for the Test match series against England. He described his first test match as 'disastrous' and it was to be three years before he was chosen again. The value of the experience was not lost on him, however, and he became more determined than ever to win back his place.

After his failure to make an impact on his first tour, he turned his attention to his education and after completing a two year A-level course in only nine months at Worcester Grammar School, he was awarded a place at Oxford University in October 1972. In the meantime, he was playing county cricket for Worcestershire but finding it difficult to settle into the life of the English county cricketer, with its emphasis on boozing and pub culture. In 1974, he was elected Oxford captain, and his form began to improve radically, he said that the responsibility of captaincy made him a better player.

Attending Keble College, Oxford, he studied Geography in his first year before switching to Politics and Economics. Whilst at University he was viewed as an aloof and somewhat arrogant individual- a characterisation which would follow him for much of his time in the public eye. This was offset, however, with his dashing Eastern good looks which gained him the reputation as something of a ladies' man, a tag with which he would be labelled until he eventually married in 1995. Khan, himself, declared rather suggestively, 'Oxford was a complete education...! enjoyed it to the full.'

In 1974, his performances for Oxford persuaded the Pakistani selectors to give him the opportunity to revive his Test career with a recall for the upcoming tour of England. In light of this, Wisden, the cricketing equivalent of the Bible, pronounced that 'he would be a powerful figure in Pakistan cricket for years to come.' The hard work and application were starting to pay off, Imran's reputation as a player to watch flourished, he was emerging as the first truly fast bowler to come out of Pakistan.

Imran was called up to play in the World Cup of 1975 which was being held in England. The opposition were Australia; the time, right in the middle of Oxford final exams. He saw this conflict of interests as a challenge. Thus, after completing two of his papers, he travelled to the game at Edgbaston on the following morning. Unfortunately for Imran and Pakistan, they lost. The effects on Imran were doubly miserable. There was not only the pain of defeat but also a bout of flu which left him in no fit state to complete his examinations.

After finishing his finals, he left Oxford in 1975 with a good second class degree in politics and a third in economics; results which his former tutor Dr Hayes believed were 'a gross injustice to his intellect.'

During 1976, he continued playing for Worcestershire, and with a hefty haul of sixty-one wickets and over a thousand runs that season, Wisden sagely noted that Imran should be 'identified as an allrounder of world-class potential.' Yet, despite his success with the team, he was unhappy living in Worcester and after a year of legal wranglings and harsh words, he was released by the county and joined Sussex County Cricket Club.

In April 1977, he was chosen to play in Kerry Packer's infamous World Series Cricket in Australia. It was this decision that kept him out of test matches for a year. However, it gave him the opportunity to play alongside fellow sporting greats such as demon fast bowlers Dennis Lillee and Michael Holding. Imran's prowess as a both bowler and batsman were cemented, and after the intervention of Pakistan President Zia, he was once again admitted into the international cricket fold.

Khan's reintroduction to test match cricket coincided with a historic test series against old rivals, India. It was during this series that Imran was to become a fully fledged star. In Karachi, his match winning knock against the Indian attack led him to be feted as a hero by his fellow countrymen. Pakistan triumphed 2-0 over the whole series and the Pakistani press and public alike put it down to Imran's efforts.

As the decidedly salacious seventies slid into the more earnest eighties, Imran's star quality began to shine brightly. He was as prevalent in the gossip columns as he was on the back pages of the National Press. In 1981, during the final test of the series with Australia, he became Pakistan's highest wicket-taker with 144 wickets to his name. It was clear that he was more than just an exceptional player. He was increasingly being viewed as someone who could lead his side to greater heights.

In 1982, he was named as Pakistan's captain, an acknowledgement that his performances and attitude merited. It was to be Imran's first period as captain and was both a personal and professional triumph. A test win over England and series victories over India and Australia showed that he had the making of a first rate captain. His performances were nothing short of dazzling. The most outstanding of these was the capture of eight wickets for sixty runs against India, the best statistics by a Pakistani against their oldest enemy. Wisden put him on a par with Ian Botham and Sir Richard Hadlee and made him one of the top five cricketers of the year.

In the meantime, his exploits off the field were to become as engrossing as his heroics on it. His charm, education, finely chiselled features, and that pervasive air of justified superiority had made him the darling of the Upper class 'Sloane Ranger' set and he was regularly seen at the plushest night-clubs including Stringfellows and Tramp. The papers quickly latched onto him and he was instantly labelled 'a playboy' for his high profile dalliances with very eligible high society beauties such as Susannah Constantine and Emma Sargeant.

He was the epitome of the strong silent type, and even though his habits were markedly different from his friends- he was a teetotaller with staunch Islamic beliefs surrounded by champagne-quaffing, caviar munching socialites- he became hugely popular. The Independent commented that he led 'a social life of extreme elegance.' Contrary to this image, Imran was quoted as saying that, I hated being a playboy...cricket was always my obsession.'

The following years, 1984 and 1985, saw events conspire against him; it was a period as painful as any he had or would experience. The course of his life would be radically altered.

During the World Cup of 1983, in which he led Pakistan to the semi finals, he picked up a nagging shin injury. This was exacerbated by continued county cricket and eventually X-rays showed he had a stress fracture of the shin bone. It was a shattering blow and doctors told him his playing days were over at the age of thirty-two. At this stage of his career, he could not be blamed for considering retirement yet his pride would not allow him the luxury. He undertook painful sessions of experimental medicine and rehabilitation, before miraculously being given the all clear in October 1984. That same year he was restored to the captaincy of his country- this was a true testament to the man's spirit. The next year, however, was to bring greater tragedy still.

As he continued his recovery from the injury that almost ended his career, Imran was devastated by the news that his beloved mother, Shaukat, had contracted terminal and inoperable cancer. Though he did all he could by bringing her to the Cromwell Hospital in London and spending most of his time with her, she died in 1985. The trauma of his mother's death and a series of visits to cancer units in Pakistan forced Khan to reassess his life. He saw the facilities available in his native land and he was disgusted - he was convinced that his mother died because, 'hospitals in Pakistan were overcrowded, dirty and very primitive.' He pledged to build a cancer hospital in his home town of Lahore. Five million dollars would have to be raised to build and maintain the centre.

The fundraising for the hospital, which was to be named after his mother, became increasingly time consuming and began to conflict with his cricket career - at the time he was quoted as saying, 'the hospital project is taking over my life and I'm glad.'

In 1987, he reached another cricketing milestone as he became only the eighth player in Test Match history to take three hundred wickets. The pressures of the hospital and the stress of first class cricket were beginning to take their toll on him, and after finishing as runners-up to West Indies in the 1987 World Cup, he announced his retirement from the game.

Having taken the decision to quit, he was not keen to go back on his word having already vowed to devote as much time as possible to the hospital. However, he was caught in a Catch-22 situation, he needed a high profile to raise money, but without test cricket, his ability to stay in the limelight was limited. This predicament coupled with a personal plea from President Zia, caused him to reconsider. As Imran said, 'I am ready to serve my nation and the game.'

As if every match, series or delivery was a matter of life or death, which in a very real sense it was, Imran Khan's cricketing achievements multiplied one after the other. In 1988, he captained Pakistan to their first victory over the West Indies, a match in which he delivered remarkable bowling figures of 7-80 and became the fourth highest wicket taker of all time. It was beyond question that he would be voted man of the series.

Khan's exploits in the field were filling the coffers of the hospital project, yet he did not have the Midas touch in every aspect of life. In 1987, he was named editor-in-chief of a monthly cricketing magazine named Cricket Life. It folded after only thirteen unlucky issues, yet Imran, who received no income for the project, only worried about the hospital project. Shahid Sadullah, editor of Cricket Life, stated that 'he (Imran) was concerned about his credibility after something he had put his name to had not done very well...he was concerned that it would affect him raising funds for the hospital.'

In 1989, he left his county team Sussex, committing himself only to the hospital and Pakistan. As he spent more and more time in his homeland, Imran devoted long hours to bring on the next generation of cricketing 'legends.' Two of these were Wasim Akram and Waqar Younis, both exceptionally talented and both future stars of the Pakistani test line-up .

He continued to captain Pakistan throughout the early nineties, but now, his time and attention were just as focused on Humanitarian issues (the cancer hospital, the plight of his people and as a special Ambassador for UNICEF in Bangladesh.) It seems, therefore, ironic that his greatest cricketing achievement was yet to come.

In 1992, the World Cup finals were to held in Australia. For Imran, it was not a question of if Pakistan could win but how and when Pakistan would win. He knew that defeat would prove a major setback to the hospital project, and moreover that victory would secure its future. The tournament started badly. One victory in five games had them written off as also-rans. Triumphs over Australia, Sri Lanka and New Zealand (twice) led them into the final against England in Melbourne. It was a tight match but when Imran finally despatched England's tail-end batsman Richard Illingworth back to the pavilion, Pakistan were world champions. The magazine, Asiaweek stated in 1997, that 'This was a feat so unexpected that even today people talk about it.' In typically philanthropic style, he donated his £85,000 prize money to the hospital appeal. The World Cup win would allow the hospital to be completed. It had taken two and a half years to raise one and a half million pounds, the very same amount was raised only six weeks after the World Cup win.

This was Imran Khan's crowning moment. lie knew that the achievement would bring some sense of cohesion to his strife ridden country. He also understood that this was the perfect time to resign from the world cricket stage. Few sportsmen retire at the very apex of their careers, most go on until they are mere shadows and their past glories often become distant memories. It showed superb judgement and self discipline for Imran to make such a decision. On his return to Pakistan, he was greeted by throngs of cheering fans - English journalist, Kate Muir, who travelled with Imran declared, 'he was received as if he were Gazza, the Beatles and President Kennedy rolled into one in a country famished for idols.' Imran had risen from conquering hero to legend. He retired at the age of thirty-nine after playing for twenty-one years.

As he retired, he proclaimed that 'my priority in life has shifted from cricket to the cancer hospital. In cricket, I have no ambition left.' Yet, life after sport has proved no less eventful for Khan.

In 1993 he was appointed to the unsalaried post of Ambassador for Tourism, his basic role being to improve the image of Pakistan around the world. It would be a tough task in a country that was desperately troubled and deeply divided. Nevertheless, he was the perfect candidate to bring some much needed good publicity.

While Imran spent more and more of his time fundraising for the hospital, his main source of income came from writing cricketing articles for the Daily Telegraph newspaper and receiving royalties from an autobiography entitled 'All

Round View' written in 1988 (it sold over 20,000 copies in its first year of publication.) In 1993, he published another book, on a subject far removed from the sporting sphere, its title 'Warrior Race' referred to the Pathan tribe, a rugged Pakistani hill dwelling tribe of whom Imran was a descendant. He spent months living with the Pathan, researching their customs and exploring his roots.

By 1995, Imran had finally fulfilled his most ambitious dream. The Shaukat Khanum Memorial Hospital and Cancer Research Centre was completed, at a cost of $10,000,000. Set in a twenty acre field outside his hometown of Lahore, it treats over sixty patients, most of those free of charge. It was an amazing achievement and its success rests squarely on the shoulders of Imran; one associate put it quite succinctly, 'the only thing working in Pakistan is his hospital.'

That year was to prove as momentous as any in Imran's memorable life. On May 16 in Paris, Imran, the long-term bachelor, was married to Jemima Goldsmith, the beautiful, blonde, 21 year old daughter of billionaire Sir James Goldsmith. The nuptials proved to be somewhat controversial. Firstly many believed that Khan should have married a Pakistani, moreover, they were concerned about her Jewish ancestry. Jemima allayed their fears by converting to Islam and changing her name to Jemila Khan. She moved to Pakistan, began to learn Urdu and spends much of her time fund-raising and running the hospital.

The following year, Imran finally made his long delayed entry into the political arena, when he launched his Movement for Justice Party, in April 1996, on a platform of reform, anti-corruption, and decentralisation of power. 'I feel Pakistan is heading for disaster...I want to bring about real change,' he explained. Though he lacked experience, his name and standing would undoubtedly be an advantage in his new career. Susan Berfield wrote in Asiaweek. 'He has a squeaky clean reputation where the leading politicians do not.' Imran's supporters say that his move into politics was purely altruistic; his opponents counter that it is ambition and blind power lust that drives him.

In the same month as the foundation of Tehreek-I-Insaaf, tragedy struck as a terrorist attack on his hospital, killed eight people and wounded thirty-eight. It was a truly cowardly assault on innocent lives and apparently was meant as a warning to Imran, yet there were no arrests and no one claimed responsibility. The attack, however, was futile in its attempt to destroy Imran or the hospital. The hospital was restored to full working order in February 1997.

On November 18, 1996, the memories of the horrendous hospital bombing were tempered by joy at the birth of his first child, Suleiman Isa. On becoming father, Imran simply said I didn't realise I would feel so much deep happiness by having a child.'

He has campaigned tirelessly since he became a politician but his successes have been limited, and it is, perhaps, too early to tell if his political work will be as illustrious as his cricketing career. The omens are not good. Former prime minister Benazir Bhutto banned all references to him and his hospital on state run television and refused to let him hold fundraising rallies as well as asking the tax department to keep a close watch on his hospital funds. These draconian measures alongside Imran's inexperience meant that his party was soundly beaten in the last election, losing their security deposits in seven constituencies. Perhaps, all is not lost. Nature has shown that this is one individual capable of making dramatic comebacks against the odds. Indeed, party insiders say that Imran, accustomed to winning on the cricket field, is becoming increasingly impatient and hungry for power in politics.

In addition to his political struggle, recent tabloid stories have tarnished the gloss of his image - he is, at present, embroiled in a paternity trial with former lover Sita White in California. He denies the accusations but it appears the judgement will go against him. There have also been reports that his marriage to Jemima, who is expecting their second child, is going through a troubled patch. It does not take a trained conspiracy theorist to realise that the reporting of these personal crises may have more than a little to do with Khan's fledgling political career.

In sporting terms, Imran proved himself to be a player without peer. As a fast bowler, he defied nature by keeping his ferocious pace after injury and age should have slowed him up considerably. Only a handful of cricketers could touch him in terms of genuine ability. None were able to match him for grace, dignity or accomplishment. In the eighties, he was largely and unwittingly responsible for doing the unthinkable and making cricket 'sexy.' Simultaneously, the cult of the cricket personality grew up-there was Ian Botham, the brash, British Jack The Lad; Vivian Richards, the smooth, laid back West Indian and Imran, the suave and mysterious playboy. It was a time when cricket reached a level of popularity, it would struggle to achieve again.

The death of his mother led him to change his outlook on life and it pushed him towards more altruistic initiatives, forsaking the personal triumphs that had been such a staple. Though his was a privileged upbringing, this was not something he fell back on. Rather, it was his unwillingness to accept setbacks and his ruthless dismissal of limitations which led him to be one of the few people who have successfully bridged the 'hero gap' between east and west. It is passion that drives him above all these -, 'everything in the world can be changed by passion.'

MALCOLM X
1925 - 1965

On February 21 1965, Malcolm X was assassinated while addressing a public meeting in Harlem, New York. It was the climatic end to a life that had captured the attentions of a world-wide audience. His transition from street hustler, thief and drug-pusher to the spokesman of the militant black organisation - the Nation of Islam - is a captivating tale. He was revered by many and reviled by many more. In a racist and turbulent America, Malcolm X was for some a prophet of black pride and consciousness; for others the unacceptable face of race-hatred and violence.

Malcolm Little was born on 19 May 1925 to a struggling black family based in Omaha, Nebraska. As with many Afro-Americans growing up in this era, Malcolm's childhood was a painful experience. Segregated, impoverished and living under the constant threat of violence, life was undoubtedly hard.

In their plight to escape racial oppression, the family moved from Omaha to Lansing, Michigan. They were dismayed to find their new neighbourhood equally racist. Once they had settled, they became the focus for a campaign of intimidation by the Ku Klux Klan. Malcolm's father was an activist who supported the United Negro Improvement Association, under the leadership of Marcus Garvey. The influence of the Ku Klux Klan in the town was made explicit when the company which sold the farmhouse to Earl and Louise Little, suddenly produced a clause prohibiting blacks from owning property. A few weeks before the family were to be evicted their house was burnt down in an arson attack. The burning down of his childhood home left a deep emotional scar on Malcolm. His sense of helplessness was only compounded as the local fire brigade stood back and watched the house bum to the ground.

The family had lost their possessions and the money they had invested in the house was never returned. In 1931, one year after they had settled in Michigan, Malcolm's father was murdered by a racist gang. The loss of his father instilled in the six year old a deep sense of grief and injustice, coupled with a burning anger to hit back against racist aggressors.

Earl Little had taken out two insurance policies to ensure his family a comfortable income in the event of his death. The first small policy of roughly £500 was paid to cover the funeral expenses, but callously the insurance company refused to pay the family any of the money from the larger policy because they had classified the death as suspicious. They then formally declared the death to be suicide. Inevitably, there were no arrests and no charges of murder. The grieving family had been cheated of their hard-earned inheritance and were forced into deeper poverty. Malcolm's mother had little option but to rely on welfare handouts. This only added to their troubles, as the welfare workers wanted to split up the family. When Malcolm was eleven, his beleaguered mother was put in a mental hospital and he was placed in a foster home.

From 1936-39, Malcolm attended junior high school. He was an intelligent, hardworking pupil, excelling at sports and becoming class president. The prodigious child had ambitions to be a lawyer, but these were shattered by teachers who advised him to go into carpentry, completely disregarding his intellectual capacity. He began to understand the inequality ingrained in US society - black people were simply not given the opportunities to excel.

In 1940, he moved to Boston to live with his half-sister, Elle. Malcolm found work as a shoeshine boy in a local night club and began to immerse himself in the city's night-life. He dropped out of school, finding full-time employment as a chef on the train service to Washington and New York. Meanwhile, Malcolm became attuned to life on the street, hustling for money and turning to petty crime. He moved to New York to pursue this questionable, if lucrative new career, robbing people and selling drugs, often under illicit influence himself. He once gave a detailed insight into this period of his life: 'During the next six to eight months, I pulled my first robberies and stickups. Only small ones. Always in other, nearby cities. And I got away. As the pros did, I would key myself up to pull these jobs by my first use of hard dope. I began with Sammy's [best friend] recommendation - sniffing cocaine.'

His criminal life-style escalated, and during the next few years in Harlem, Malcolm ran into serious trouble. In retrospect, he conceded that he was extremely fortunate not to have been shot dead by other hustlers, or to have perpetrated a killing himself. He was hunted down by notorious criminals and chased through the streets by Italian mobsters in a case of mistaken identity. A man fitting Malcolm's description had robbed the Italians at a gambling table; due to his reputation as a 'stick-up man' he became their chief suspect. The police also suspected Malcolm of numerous offences. He was fast becoming one of the most wanted men in Harlem.

Fearing his luck would run out, Malcolm parted company with New York and returned to Boston. His exploits had become notorious in his former hunting ground, and with his new-found fame and status, a continuing life of crime was too strong a lure to resist. He was soon out of control: 'Looking back, 1 think I really was at least slightly out of my mind. I viewed narcotics as most people regard food. I wore guns as today I wear my neckties. Deep down, I actually believed that after living as fully as humanly possible, one should then die violently. I expected then, as I still expect today, to die at any time. But then, I think 1 deliberately invited death in many, sometimes insane ways.'

Inevitably his criminal activities caught up with him. In 1946 he was arrested for possession of stolen goods and sentenced to ten years in jail. His two accomplices, both white girls, received one year's probation. Malcolm believed the severity of his sentence - technically it was his first offence - was the result of his relationship with the white women. Interracial relationships were not acceptable, as Malcolm found to his cost.

When Malcolm was locked up in Charlestown Prison he was still only twenty-one. The primitive living conditions combined with his anger towards his harsh sentencing, turned him into a violent and bitter inmate. He was regularly in trouble with the guards and frequently placed in isolation; other prisoners kept clear, believing him to be insane. Malcolm was nicknamed 'Satan' - an indication of his extreme behaviour.

After a few years, and at the persistent requests of Elle, Malcolm was transferred to a prison with better facilities, including a library. This experience marked a major cross-roads in his life. Malcolm underwent a transformation from wayward youth to man of education and vision. It was during his time in prison that he came across the teachings of Elijah Mohammed and his organisation - the Nation of Islam. Malcolm was keen to gain the self-control and discipline the movement seemed to offer. He taught himself to read and write so that he could write to Elijah Mohammed and learn more about his teachings. For the rest of his time in prison he studied feverishly night and day.

Seven years after his incarceration, a very changed man was released from jail. He moved to Detroit and joined the Nation of Islam. The NOI was a new movement agitating for the political, social and religious rejuvenation of black America. It was based on a controversial theology preaching that whites were the creation of a mad scientist named Yacoub. One day the white race would be destroyed, restoring the blacks to their natural glory. More immediately, the movement called for a separate black state within America. Yet, its more extreme beliefs were tempered by its attempts to reform criminals and invest in poverty-stricken areas. It promoted self-respect and pride in black heritage, at a time when many blacks felt abandoned by their state. On the whole it was perceived in a negative light by the public, reports tending to focus on its racist doctrines and anti-Semitic sermons.

The majority of black Americans at the time were of a Christian background and looked upon the NOI with disdain; others involved in the civil rights movement regarded integration not separation as the ultimate goal. Malcolm, convinced that his leader had the answers to the problems of the black community, was keen to encourage new recruits and win the group a higher profile. He spent two years in Detroit before moving to the New York branch of the organisation. During this time he reinvented himself and put his life of crime behind him. His change in attitude was accompanied by a change of name: Malcolm Little became Malcolm X. He explained that he had abandoned his 'slave name'; 'X' would refer to his lost African name and the faded heritage of the Afro-American people. An inspiring and eloquent spokesman, Malcolm's stature within the movement grew, and many new recruits were attracted. New NOI meeting places began to appear throughout the US.

The charismatic Malcolm X came into the spotlight of the national media due to the 'Hinton Incident' in 1956. He had received news that NOI member, Charles Hinton, had been beaten and detained by police despite being an innocent passer-by at a disturbance. Malcolm assembled a hundred NOI 'security guards' and marched them to the police station. The guards followed his instructions to remain silent while he went inside to demand a meeting with Hinton; he also demanded that the man should be taken to hospital to receive medical attention. The police were overwhelmed by the size, discipline and precision of the operation. One police officer famously declared of Malcolm X: 'No one man should have so much power.' The 'Hinton Incident' established Malcolm X as a powerful and respected figure within the New York black community and beyond. It also struck fear in to the minds of police and the white public in general.

During the early 1960s Malcolm X became a notorious figure in American life and a controversial alternative to Martin Luther King's civil rights movement. His distinctive, rousing speeches and direct attitude against oppression made him an extremely difficult man to ignore. He knew that many people outside the NOI wanted him to fail, but remained convinced that his cause was just. He stuck to his convictions that there was only one way to fight racism and that was to meet it head on. In response to suggestions of a less combative approach he once remarked: 'Give me a .45 calibre, then I'll sing "We Shall Overcome" (civil rights anthem).'

Malcolm learned to handle the media with a politician's caution and cunning. He had to be very careful about what he said in public as reporters would be hanging on every word, eager to turn his rhetoric against him. On one occasion a reporter attempted to provoke him into saying something 'newsworthy', asking 'Docs the black man hate the white man?' Malcolm turned the tables, denying the newsman any simplistic headline, by replying: 'That's like asking the victim of rape if she hates the person who raped her, or a wolf asking the sheep if it hates him. The White man is in no moral position to accuse anyone else of hate.'

As Malcolm X became more established and more of a celebrity, he came to feel that certain sections within the NOI were jealous of his fame. He began to sense that there were enemies within his black Muslim movement as well as outside.

The assassination of President Kennedy in 1963 shocked the nation. When interviewed shortly after the shooting, Malcolm made a rare error, giving off the record remarks to a reporter. An incredulous Malcolm X woke to the headline 'Malcolm says the President got what he deserved.' Repercussions amid a nation in mourning were hardly favourable. What Malcolm had actually said was: 'What happened was the result of a climate of hate. It's a case of the chickens coming home to roost.' His quote had been misinterpreted and he took pains to clarify his meaning: 'I said that the hate in white men had not stopped with the killing of defenceless black people, but that hate, allowed to spread unchecked, finally had struck down this country's Chief of State.' But it was too late, the damage had been done.

Malcolm X was aware that he too could become a target for an assassin's bullet. He felt under attack from all sides. The NOI issued a statement disowning him, saying that he did not speak for the black Muslim community and that his views were not shared by either their leader or his followers. After a ninety day censorship the NOI issued another statement promising reinstatement to Malcolm X - 'it he submits'. To the NOI rank and file this gave the impression that Malcolm had rebelled. To Malcolm it seemed like a set up. Three days later he heard that one of his senior assistants was telling certain members, 'If you knew what the Minister did, you'd go out and kill him yourself. Malcolm concluded that 'any death-talk for me could have been approved of - if not actually initiated - by only one man.' He believed that he had been betrayed by his leader, the Honourable Elijah Muhammed.

Malcolm X left the NOI and travelled to the Muslim holy city of Mecca where he underwent a spiritual awakening, converting to orthodox Islam, and appropriating another new name - El Hajj Malik Shabazz. He then travelled through Africa on a public speaking tour. His philosophy had now matured, and for the first time in his life there was an air of calm about him. He had survived the lowest ebb of his spiritual career. His philosophy and less hostile perception of whites had been distanced from the extremism of the NOI, but his commitment to equal rights remained undiminished.

In the summer of 1964, America was a war zone, with rioting in the major cities by blacks. Meanwhile in the South, blacks were still being lynched by white gangs. On his return to the US, Malcolm established the Organisation of Afro-American Unity. If his outlook had mellowed somewhat, this was not immediately evident from the declaration: 'We believe in self-defence by any means necessary.' It was interpreted by many whites as a call to continue the rioting, and was used by others to suggest that Malcolm was attempting to incite a 'race war'. One commentator dubbed him 'the only Negro who can stop a race war...or start one.'

No matter how the media stereotyped Malcolm X, the man himself was perfectly able to change tack and modify his approach. His decision to move on from his NOI days was illustrated when he met Martin Luther King. They both acknowledged that their polarised views on race relations had become counterproductive to the wider struggle. Malcolm reiterated this to the media: 'Our methods differ but we are both in the same battle.'

At the end of the year he attempted to take the US to the World Court of Human Rights. He failed in his bid to make the US Congress answerable for the crimes committed against blacks since the abolition of slavery. Malcolm struggled on in defiance. In the face of adversity he continued to address meetings and lectures where he preached his philosophy.

During the last few years of his life he received countless death threats, many from within the NOI. In January 1965, the NOI sent out a newsletter which contained a message that all traitors to the organisation would be silenced. It was clear to Malcolm that somebody wanted him out of the picture.

On the 19 February 1965, his home was firebombed. Thirty years had passed since his childhood home had been burnt down by a racist gang in a bid to silence his father's views, now history had come full circle. On numerous occasions he expressed the feeling that his time was up: 'I'm already a dead man,' 'It won't be long now. The end is near. He sensed that, like his father, he would have to make the ultimate sacrifice for his beliefs.

Two days after the firebombing, Malcolm X was shot dead by three black men while addressing a meeting in Harlem. There have been persistent rumours linking his death to both the CIA and the FBI, but over the years the NOI has been viewed with the most suspicion. They continue to deny any involvement in his death.

Malcolm has been variously described as a politician, a prophet, and 'the angriest man in America'. He preferred to see himself as an 'independent leader among black people.' He certainly possessed natural leadership qualities, carrying influence throughout all sections of the black community. He once alluded to this unique position: 'The point I am making is that, as a 'leader', I could talk over the ABC, CBS, or NBC microphones, at Harvard or Tuskegee; I could talk to the so-called 'middle-class' Negro and with the ghetto blacks whom all the other leaders just talked about.'

In a memorial speech in Malcolm's honour, Jack Barnes, reminded the audience of his friend's legacy: 'Malcolm asked the Black American: Who taught you to hate yourself? Who taught you to be a pacifist? Was he a pacifist? Who said Black people cannot defend themselves? Docs he defend himself? Who taught you not to go too far and too fast in your fight for freedom?' Barnes knew that due to his friend's unflinching crusade, such questions would remain firmly on the agenda for future generations.

The name Malcolm X is still synonymous with controversy and pride. For many he is an icon, epitomising black resistance to intolerable conditions. His critics are probably less vociferous than during his lifetime, but, for some, his memory is tainted with separatism, violence and some of the more extreme beliefs of the Nation of Islam. Yet, to question his methods is not erase his obvious moral courage and commitment to his cause. His life was one of colossal shifts: from criminal and prisoner to militant intellectual. Arguments recur about the importance of his late conversion to a more moderate political stance. Perhaps, one of his most positive legacies is that a willingness to question and change one's beliefs can be a sign of strength rather than weakness.

JAMES DYSON
1947 - PRESENT DAY

The Dyson Dual Cyclone was launched in 1993. Five years later it became the biggest selling vacuum cleaner on the British market, pushing the company's turnover to £100 million in the UK and almost £2 billion world-wide. From 1993 to 1998 the company was Britain's fastest growing manufacturer, also becoming the first in its field to export to Japan, the undisputed world leader in electrical goods. This impressive catalogue of success is the result of one man's persistence. James Dyson headed Enterprise Magazine's 1998 list of the UK's top entrepreneurs. His wealth is estimated at £400 million. His fascinating biography Against The Odds portrays a determined dreamer and illustrates how a talented and focused individual can prove the doubters wrong.

James Dyson was born in Norfolk in 1947. He was raised in a large Victorian house on the site of Gresham's Public School, where his father was a Classics master. He describes an idyllic early childhood, roaming the vast tracks of local countryside and coastal sand dunes with his friends.

This idyllic existence was shattered when he was just nine. In 1956, his father lost a three year battle against cancer. The traumatic event engendered feelings of isolation and independence. He comments, 'Life became something I had to make up as I went along, and I had to work everything out for myself. In crass, psychoanalytic terms, I suppose it made me a fighter.' When he played games against the older members of his family he was always up against people who were bigger and stronger than he was. He explains - 'I was not prepared to lose everything all the time just because I was the youngest - [it] taught me that I could take on something much bigger than I was, and win. Combined with the loss of my father, this made me very competitive.' The experience of being the underdog and battling against more powerful opposition would prove fundamental to later life.

At the tender age of ten, Dyson stepped forward before his boarding school peers and volunteered to play the bassoon. Actually, he had no idea what a bassoon was, but he was willing to try. Dyson believes that this event was a watershed in his life. He had demonstrated the will to challenge himself, and he would later demonstrate the concentration and dedication necessary to meet the challenge. Throughout his formative years he would strive to overcome many more obstacles.

The decision to take up running was another example of his need to test and improve himself. Once again he took the challenge very seriously: 'I would get up at six in the morning and run off into the wilds of Norfolk for hours, or put on my running kit at ten o'clock at night and not reappear until after midnight. Out there alone on the dunes I got a terrific buzz from knowing that I was doing something that no one else was - they were all tucked up in bed at boarding school.'

Dyson was determined to do things his way. Even as a youth he would reproach those who poured scorn on his ideas. He learnt that he could profit from approaching problems from an original perspective. He would carry this valuable lesson into adulthood, especially in the creation of designs that would break the mould.

He did not excel at O-Levels, but surprised many with the decision not to follow his father's footsteps into teaching. Instead, he announced his future would be in art and design. In 1966, he moved to London to study at Byam Shaw Art School. On arrival in the capital, he felt something of an outsider or as he put it, 'a country yokel,' yet it was this feeling of isolation that would set him apart and put him on his path to later achievements. During this foundation course he met his future wife, Deirdre Hindmarsh. He reflects fondly upon this period in his life: 'The Byam Shaw Art School gave me pretty much everything I have now. I had met the woman who would not only share my life, but make possible all the professional things that I did, and provide the strength to see me through the desperate years of struggle.'

After completing the course, he accepted a place at the prestigious Royal College of Art. While studying at the RCA he became inspired by the great designers and engineers of the past. In particular, the English engineer Isambard Kingdom Brunel, and the American inventor Buckminster Fuller caught his attention. He aspired to be as influential and devoted to his work as his heroes. The two inventors made him realise that simply being a designer was not enough; one had to be the complete package. This is Dyson's 'holistic' theory of design, as he explains: 'I had to master not only engineering but, product design, finance, management, and be sure that when the time came, I would be able to take my vision - whatever it may be - to completion entirely on my own. I would have to be a new kind of Brunel. Rougher, tougher, sharper than before.'

While still at the RCA, Dyson was given the opportunity to help out on a project to build a theatre at Stratford East. He seized the moment and begged the theatre group to let him design it for them. Dyson's typically idiosyncratic idea was for a theatre which would be functional yet eye-catching - he drew up blueprints for a mushroom shaped structure constructed from aluminium. With his design approved he went excitedly to British Aluminium to see if they would supply the material. Their response was one of sheer ridicule. He was mockingly advised to try his idea out on Jeremy Fry (the millionaire managing director of Rotork, a design and manufacturing company). With this rejection still burning and with nothing to lose, he took a chance and attempted to meet Fry: 'I had simply dialled directory enquiries and asked for Jeremy Fry's phone number. And he invited me to his house for supper.' Fry did not fund his aluminium theatre, but he did offer him a job. Dyson describes Fry as a modern day Isambard Brunel, single-minded and happy to swim against the tide of tradition. On a more personal level, Dyson was married to Deidre in 1968 and in 1971 their first child Emily was born.

In the forthcoming years Dyson gained priceless experience working for Rotork. His breakthrough arrived in 1970, with his design for the Sea Truck: a small, sophisticated, lightweight boat that could carry bulk objects and moor on beaches from the water. Initially, the Sea Truck appeared to be faltering, until Dyson's revision of the marketing strategy brought about results. With this innovation he won contracts with several countries, including a multi-million pound deal with the Libyan Navy. The twenty-five-year-old art student was starting to make waves. His down-to-earth yet ambitious character was ideally suited to the world of design engineering.

With his profits from the Sea Truck, Dyson and his wife bought a farm house in Badminton, situated in the Cotswolds. There was much renovation to be done, and lacking the funds to employ builders, they undertook the repairs themselves. The farm house proved to be a great inspiration to invention. During the renovation, Dyson was struck by the idea of a 'Ballbarrow'. He had spent a lot of time fumbling around the backyard trying to push his heavy and unstable wheelbarrow around in the mud. There had to be a better design; Dyson went back to basics to reinvent the wheel. By simply replacing the wheel with a large plastic ball to enable the barrow to pass over any terrain, and altering the design and material of the container to prevent the contents slopping over the side, he created a lighter and more efficient garden tool. The Ballbarrow convinced him to make the break with Rotork and produce his own inventions.

In 1974, attempting to drum up investment and support for the project, he visited ICI to discuss the feasibility of the Ballbarrow. ICI were unimpressed, but typically this only strengthened the resolve of the young designer. In order to get his product off the ground he needed to raise some capital, so he went into partnership with his brother-in-law, Stuart Kirkwood. In the late 1970s they launched the invention. Never one for gimmicks or quirks, Dyson based the design on utility and simplicity. The Ballbarrow was a great success, taking over 70 per cent of the domestic wheelbarrow market in a few months; nevertheless, it was not all plain sailing. Spurred by the national success of the product and hungry for a slice of the world market, the board handling the affairs of the newly formed Kirk-Dyson sent their new sales manager to America to meet interested parties. Instead of promoting Dyson's interests, the manager, selfishly, promoted his own, returning to announce that he had landed a new job. The betrayal hurt the company financially and Dyson personally, but the worst was yet to come. Not only was he leaving, he had also given the Ballbarrow idea to his new company, Glassco, who were putting their own version into production. The board insisted on a lawsuit; Dyson argued that it would be too expensive a risk; they would not relent.

By late 1978, the lawsuit was not going well and the costs were rising. More arguments broke out. Dyson was pushed to the fringes of a board who began to take greater cuts out of the business. He believed he was being ousted from the company due to creative jealousy, myopia and small-mindedness. Finally, he was forced out of Kirk-Dyson. To add to his woes, he lost the rights to the Ballbarrow on a technicality: naively he had placed the patent under the company name rather than his own. It taught him another valuable lesson: never lose control of your invention.

During the lawsuit Dyson's mother died, also from cancer. Now both his parents were gone and he had been ousted from his own company. It was a low point in his personal and professional life. However, it was not in his nature to quit.

While still working on the Ballbarrow, Dyson had noticed that the air-filter in the spray finishing room seemed to be consistently clogged with powder particles from the paint. He set about remedying the problem with characteristic drive and diligence. Dyson believed the solution lay in cyclone technology which could remove the powder particles by centrifugal force. Thus, he constructed a cyclone tower which span the extracted air at the speed of sound. While cleaning his house, he found that his old cleaner was also becoming blocked in much the same way as the air-filter.

Could the cyclone principle work for vacuum cleaners as well? He had stumbled on an idea that would make his fortune.

Dyson knew he would encounter the usual scepticism towards a new idea. The initial response suggested that he would have to struggle just to get people to take him seriously. He vividly recalls the early reactions: 'It must have been sometime in 1979 that I first heard the words, "But James, if there was a better kind of vacuum cleaner Hoover or Electrolux would have invented it." ' By 1982, he was seriously wondering whether his invention would ever see the light of day. He had approached every European vacuum cleaner manufacturer all to no avail. Dyson believes they were all too preoccupied with an automatic defence of their own products, to listen to reason. His only option was to seek a licence from an American or Japanese company. The big American firms were interested but refused to promise Dyson a fair share of the profits.

Finally, in 1985, after producing 5,127 prototypes, a deal was struck. The Japanese company Apex agreed to manufacture a cleaner similar to the Cyclone, with Dyson in charge of design. The cleaner known as the 'G-Force' - went on to make sales of over £12 million over the next few years, although Dyson only received £60,000 a year in royalties. It was more than a purely financial success, winning the International Design Fair prize in Japan. In fact, the machine became something of a status symbol, selling at £1,200 apiece. Buoyed by his achievements in the Far East, he was still keen to manufacture his Dual Cyclone cleaner for European and American markets.

The arduous task of finding a manufacturer was, by now, depressingly familiar. A company would show great interest in his design, complications would arise, and the deal would fall through. A clear example of this had taken place in 1983 with Black & Decker. They were keen to sign an agreement but refused to provide any money upfront. Dyson was appalled by such short-sightedness: 'Pathetic, isn't it? For a gigantic corporation to quibble with a small inventor over a few dollars, expecting him, rather than themselves, to take financial responsibility should the project fail.' When negotiations with another interested company, Conair, broke down, Dyson cursed his luck. By coincidence, Paul L. Lemer, the man who had scuppered the deal at Black & Decker, had moved to Conair, where again he was assigned responsibility to Dyson's proposals.

Dyson was learning about business the hard way. Of the deals he did clinch during the Eighties, he believed that the companies were abusing their power and trying to undermine his control over his invention. In 1991 Dyson fought two major lawsuits, one against Amway and another against Vax. Both companies were giants in their respective markets, but if Dyson was intimidated he did not show it. He continued to fight and his doggedness eventually allowed him to settle both disputes. At the time he was under immense stress, with financial pressures building against his relentless drive to get his cleaner onto the market.

As usual Dyson was forced to go it alone. By 1991 he was ready to attempt production of the Dual Cyclone for the British market, but still needed to raise £750,000. With a typically negative response from the banks, he decided to borrow the money himself, rather than get a loan through his company. He eventually raised the funds with his houses in Bath and Chelsea as security. He obviously had the confidence in his abilities to take considerable financial risks. His confidence was well founded.

In June 1993, he opened his own research centre and factory in Wiltshire, and developed a machine that collected even finer particles (down to the microscopic particles that cause allergies). The result was the DC01, the first range of models which boasted 100 percent suction all the time. The Dual Cyclone system was the first break through in vacuum cleaner technology since its invention in 1901. As a product it was highly efficient, as a design it was a classic. A testament to its good looks, the Dyson Dual Cyclone is on permanent display in design museums throughout Europe, Japan and America.

Once production of the Cyclone was underway he sought to establish connections with retailers. Yet, many chose to freeze him out of the market in deference to more established clients and their products. Dyson had to convince them that his product would sell. He first sold to home-shopping catalogues, such as Great Universal Stores and Littlewoods. Sales grew over the next two years but he knew that fifty per cent of the market was being excluded from him. Eventually, consumer power won through, retailers simply could not ignore the Cyclone's popularity. To its designer's delight, it became Britain's best selling cleaner. Its distinctive yellow and silver design was so eye-catching that it was an instant influence to other manufacturers. Hoover, Electrolux and Miele who all brought out similar looking machines - the public, however, were not fooled.

After his many arduous struggles, the future looks bright for Dyson and his company. A combination of exceptional design and engineering, coupled with a solid business philosophy which incorporates, amongst other things, a youthful creative staff and a policy of top to bottom office equality, have provided the company with a solid foundation for the next millennium.

Dyson remains a man of steadfast principles. He believes he is now in a position to fight for the rights of fellow inventors and designers. An example of this is the legal suit that he is currently pursuing against the Department of Trade and Industry. He is taking them to the European Court of Human Rights over patent protection. Of the action, Dyson says with typical candour, 'if [you] can't afford an annual renewal fee, you lose your patent. The establishment figure that this will stop people from sitting on a technological breakthrough, this is patent rubbish. It stacks the odds in favour of the corporations, it's a human rights issue.'

Without his endless reserves of perseverance, self-belief and dedication, Dyson's triumph would have been impossible. Single-minded to the point of obstinacy, he never allowed the large corporations to dominate him or belittle his ideas. Utility and ingenuity were pitted against the might (and often complacency) of the big corporations. Dyson clearly revels in his hard-fought victory: 'I took on the big boys at their own game, made them look silly, just by being true to myself.' His instinct to go against the grain, instilled at an early age, has come up against innumerable boundaries. Yet, his idiosyncrasies held the key to success, proving that originality is, indeed, a priceless commodity. Despite the brilliance behind his designs, his philosophy is really quite simple: 'I'd like to think my inventions have had as important an impact as Fuller's or Brunei's - inventions should be made to make life easier.' This simple maxim goes a long way to explaining why all James Dyson's hard work has not been in vain.

MARGARET THATCHER
1925 - 2013

Margaret Hilda Thatcher has left an indelible mark (some might call it a stain) on the political landscape of British history. From a humble provincial background she broke into the political elite, initiating a career which would take her to the leadership of the Conservative Party and beyond. In 1979, she became her country's first woman premier. By the time she left 10 Downing Street in 1990, she had become her century's longest serving Prime Minister, winning three consecutive general elections. Her father was a source of inspiration and influence; his values established the foundations of her philosophy and continued to inform her decisions. Thatcher's brand of unapologetic Conservatism won countless devotees and enemies on a global scale. Her defiant, battling image persists in the public consciousness; her power may have waned, but her influence lives on.

Margaret Roberts was born above the family grocery store in Grantham, Lincolnshire on 13 October 1925. She was the second daughter of a thrifty Methodist couple who had taken out a mortgage to buy their own shop. Her childhood was active and pleasurable despite a home-life she described as 'practical, serious and intensely religious'. If fun was not a sin, idleness certainly was. A sense of duty and purpose pervaded a household in which the customer always came first. She was educated in the virtues of good house-keeping and efficient shop-keeping. Her early years were rigorously structured and organized. An aptitude for organization would prove essential to future challenges. She would later pay tribute to the source of this talent: 'it was from my mother that I inherited the ability to organize and combine so many different duties of an active life.'

A love of politics, reading and intellectual debate was fostered early by her father. Alfred Roberts was a self-taught scholar, lay preacher and local councillor. He was a deeply principled man whose forthright views and cherished values were to have a profound effect on his daughter. One of his favourite sayings was 'Never do things just because other people do them.' An intrinsic sense of self-reliance and self-belief would be evident throughout his daughter's career, especially in her willingness to face down critics and adhere to her principles. She later acknowledged a debt to the 'upright qualities' of her father 'which entailed a refusal to alter your convictions just because others disagreed or because you became unpopular'. In later life the preacher's daughter would learn to live with unpopularity. Perhaps her father's combination of religion and politics assured her of the righteousness as well as the rightness of her own opinions.

She fought her first general election in 1935 aged ten, folding leaflets and running information for the local Tory candidate. An education at Huntingtower Road Primary School then Kesteven and Grantham Girl's School was supplemented by her father's enthusiasm for the Classics, especially Kipling, and devotion to current affairs. However, despite her interest in literature and politics, Margaret chose to specialize in chemistry. If this was perhaps a surprising choice for an aspiring politician, the decision to target Oxford University was less so. At seventeen she was distraught when she failed to gain a scholarship to Somerville College. Yet, the set-back was short-lived; a telegram brought fortuitous news: someone had dropped out and a place was available. Not for the last time luck was on her side - if acceptance had arrived any later than 1943 she would have been restricted to a 'wartime degree' and eligible for national service.

A sheltered childhood made for a rather shy and awkward freshman in the overpowering confines of Oxford. In the liberated atmosphere of student life she tried her first cigarette - only to conclude that a daily copy of the Times would prove a shrewder investment. There was to be no personal rebellion against the tenets of her upbringing. In fact, most of her extra-curricular activities centred around the Oxford University Conservative Association, of which she became Treasurer and then President. This was to prove another shrewd investment as it allowed her to rub shoulders with the great and good of the Conservative Party, including Prime Minister to be, Anthony Eden. Her time at Oxford was more significant for her political education than for the second-class chemistry degree she graduated with.

In the 1945 general election campaign, the student cut her teeth in the art of political oratory. Supporting candidates at home and in Oxford, she took to the stage as a warm-up speaker, learning to think on her feet and field questions from a critical audience. The resolute, booming intonation that would in future years dominate the House of Commons can be traced back to these early forays. No doubt a recollection of childhood sermons as well as formal elocution lessons aided her oratorical development. Yet, on this occasion all her efforts were in vain; the Labour Party won a famous landslide while Tory hopefuls were decimated. She was dismayed by this treatment of Conservative leader, Winston Churchill, whose war-time radio broadcasts had been such a revelation to her. In 1983, after the Falklands War, a Prime Minister would demonstrate just how to translate a military success into an electoral victory.

By the lime she left Oxford the ambitious graduate had Westminster in her sights. However, pecuniary considerations had to prevail; and Ms Roberts had to find work. Interviews came and went. On one occasion she spied on her ICI interviewer's notes to read: 'This young woman has much too strong a personality to work here.' The young woman was subsequently taken on by BX Plastics. Yet, as always her thoughts were on politics and she was keen to advertise her ambition. Her perseverance paid dividends when an Oxford acquaintance put in a good word with the Chairman of the Dartford Conservative Association. Doubts arising over the suitability of a woman to stand for Parliament were put aside, and she was duly selected to fight the constituency in the 1950 general election. (Husband-in-waiting Denis Thatcher was a member of the candidate selection panel.) The Kent seat was not considered winnable and on two attempts she was unsuccessful. Nonetheless, on both occasions she fought impressive campaigns and gained substantial votes. She was not an MP, but her political verve did not go unnoticed.

In December 1951, she celebrated the start of a long happy marriage to Denis. He was the dashing, Jaguar-driving, jet-setting manager of the family paint business. When they returned from a honeymoon in Madeira, the couple moved into Denis' Chelsea flat. Mrs Thatcher adored her new role as a wife, moving in affluent circles, and holidaying in Paris and Rome. It was all a far cry from childhood holidays in Skegness; yet there was further to climb for the Grantham girl, even with two career obstacles waiting around the corner. The twins, Mark and Carol, were born in 1953. For a less ambitious, determined, and (now) wealthy mother this might have spelt the end of a promising career. However, with the assistance of a nanny and her own inbred adroitness at organizing a hectic lifestyle, Maggie battled on.

After the Dartford disappointments, she decided on a change of direction; leaving the job she had taken as a food analyst for J. Lyons & Co, she began to study law. She took her Bar finals in the same year the twins arrived and went into practice as a tax lawyer. An experience of law and its rhetorical demands ineluctably drew her attention back to her primary passion. Robustly weathering criticism about the role of a wife and mother, Thatcher finally secured selection for a safe Tory seat. She became MP for Finchley in 1959.

The family moved into 'Dormers', a large detached house at Farnborough in Kent. The new parliamentarian cherished her country garden - a luxury she had always dreamed about. If there was a British equivalent to the American Dream, Thatcher had achieved it. But the rural housewife had to cohabit with the determined politician. Her struggle to maintain both roles was eased when the twins were sent to boarding school; yet, her appetite for work would remain insatiable. As Prime Minister she would learn to subsist on four hours sleep a night. Interestingly, her loyalty to traditional values would distance her achievements from any feminist agenda. 'I owe nothing to Women's Lib,' she declared years later to the Observer (1 December 1974).

The fledgling MP made a prodigious start to her parliamentary career. Her tenacious debating style was well tailored to the adversarial system of British politics, as was her proclivity to hold strong opinions. She also made her mark on Macmillan's left-leaning government by voting in favour of a proposal to introduce the birching of young offenders. She was, in short, the archetypal 'conviction politician' whose assured sense of right and wrong would become synonymous with strong leadership in an uncertain world.

The entrenched will to avoid complacency was crucial to Thatcher's success in Parliament. When she was appointed to her first government post as junior minister for pensions in 1960, she was determined not to be railroaded into a cosy compliance with the official line. She stubbornly refused to sign letters or accept answers without a detailed explanation from her officials. This approach ensured access to priceless information and allowed her to exercise real authority and control. She quickly gained a reputation for faultless preparation and attention to detail. It was an approach she would bring to her numerous appointments.

In 1970, Conservative Prime Minister Edward Heath appointed her Secretary of State for Education and Science. Again she was at odds with officialdom, finding her department too left-wing and too close to the teaching unions. In an environment she regarded as 'self-righteously socialist' she pursued an executive rather than consultative style. Her approach was at odds with a Prime Minister she came to view as tainted with collectivism and compromise. Heath, in turn, disapproved of the undemocratic style in which she ran her department. He recently claimed: '(instead of explaining her views to her senior officials she simply marched in with a list of demands she expected them to carry out without question.' The two were never close. In her eyes he was obsessed with European integration, and lacked the monetarist economic credentials of her only cabinet friend and long-term mentor, Sir Keith Joseph. Together they would map out a very different path, with a focus on individual enterprise rather than any collective good.

Initial triumphs at the DES turned sour when the ostensibly dormant issue of school milk became volatile. In order to make savings in the education budget, the legal obligation to provide milk was dropped. 'Mrs Thatcher, Milk Snatcher' shrieked the headlines. In 1971 The Sun voted her 'The Most Unpopular Woman in Britain'. She was 'hurt and upset' by the campaign against her, and soon stopped reading personal profiles in the newspapers. If Mrs Thatcher had a sensitive and vulnerable side it became subsumed beneath an impregnable exterior. Her tough and uncompromising media image became ubiquitous. While it would become her greatest asset, it would also enable her detractors to characterize her outlook as devoid of compassion and sensitivity.

When Heath failed to win the 1974 general election, Thatcher swapped her ministerial car for a Vauxhall Viva, and concluded it was time for a fundamental rethink. Unsatisfied with her leader's performance, she backed Keith Joseph's Centre for Policy Studies, which aimed to put free-enterprise principles into practice. Initially it was her intention to support Joseph in a bid for the leadership, but after the fallout from a disastrous speech at Edgbaston he informed her of his decision not to mount a challenge. It required little encouragement for Thatcher to realize her chance had arrived. Buoyed by the support of colleagues (impressed with her muscular performances in the House) she fought tooth and nail for control of the party. On 4 February 1975 she defeated a bitter Heath in the first leadership ballot. He has recently claimed that Thatcher's triumph in the contest was due to the shrewd manoeuvring of her campaign manager, Airey Neave. According to Heath, Neave told MPs he didn't expect Thatcher to do well in the first round but encouraged them to vote for her simply to limit Heath's majority. In the event, Thatcher won the first round by 130 votes to Heath's 119. He took up the role of attacking Thatcher at every opportunity; she took charge of the Conservative Party.

She found her time as Leader of the Opposition (1975-79) both frustrating and informative. In the Commons she faced the political expertise of Harold Wilson and later Jim Callaghan. Even against the latter's ailing and unpopular coalition government, she was unable to force an election and satisfy her ambition for the top job. Conversely, this period allowed her to make numerous trips abroad. Personal meetings with the notorious Romanian dictator, Nicolae Ceausescu, confirmed her suspicion of Communism. Visits to the United States reaffirmed her confidence in the free-market. She was warmly received by the US, where she first met Ronald Reagan in 1975. As future President, he would be a key ally to her cause. She would always expound the value of Britain's 'special relationship' with the US - which she clearly favoured to Britain's uncertain position within the EEC. Her journeys corroborated her long-held view that 'communism was the regime of the privileged elite, capitalism the creed for the common man.'

Her pro-American rhetoric was more than matched by the venom she levelled against the Soviet Union. In a spate of speeches she emphasized that Communism posed a real military danger, not merely a political difference. After one such outburst, the Soviet Red Star christened her 'The Iron Lady'. Gordon Reece, a trusted media adviser, was quick to spot the potential of the comment. Thatcher was quick to catch on: '(they had inadvertently put me on a pedestal as their strongest European opponent. They never did me a greater favour.' To ensure full advantage had been taken, she was photographed a few days later driving a tank. Reece, a former television producer, proved an inspired choice of advisor; he was also instrumental in the decision to forge closer links with the tabloid press. They were more than happy to rally round the notion of a strong patriotic leader they caricatured as 'The Iron Lady', 'Battling Maggie' and 'Atilla the Hen'.

In consultation with her advisors, Thatcher set about restructuring the aims and values of the party. She sought to promote enterprise by withdrawing state involvement in the private sector; control inflation through the supply of money into the economy; and, tackle the inefficiency of the public sector, partly through 'privatisation'. Some traditional Tories were sceptical of the new direction, preferring a more interventionist approach. Conservatives who belonged to this school of thought were labelled 'Wets' by Thatcher, as opposed to the 'Dries' who shared her philosophy. Other values that characterized her leadership were a strong sense of patriotism, the importance of the family unit, the work ethic and the necessity of law and order.

Thatcher knew that the 1979 general election was her big chance. If unsuccessful, she was convinced that she would not be given another opportunity. Her victory was based on her usual combination of will power, resilience and good fortune. She would later concede that if the election had been called a year earlier, as widely predicted, it might have been her government rather than the Labour Party that was destroyed by the 'winter of discontent' (1978- 79). This proliferation of strikes which brought the country to a standstill, in fact, played right into her hands. Her long held wish to curb the powers of trade unions now translated into a vote-winner. She resisted calls from colleagues and Central Office to moderate her approach, and fought the elections on her political principles.

As she triumphantly stood on the steps of No. 10 for the first time as Prime Minister, on May 14 1979, she quoted a prayer of St. Francis of Assisi beginning, 'Where there is discord, may we bring harmony.' However, harmony was not the most applicable term for her eleven year reign.

Thatcher's first year in government was a distinctly bumpy ride. After a massive increase in unemployment and a rise in the value of the pound, she was immediately under pressure to reappraise her policies. Remaining steadfast, as ever, she made a defiant conference speech containing her famous quip: 'You turn if you like. The lady's not for turning.' After an uncertain start, she began to implement the policies that were to take Britain into a new political climate. The first major assault on the trade unions came in 1982 with legislation outlawing secondary strikes and giving employers greater freedom to dismiss employees. It wasn't long before Thatcherite 'progress' incurred the wrath of liberals, left-wingers and even traditional Tories. Her 1981 immigration legislation was considered draconian by many commentators. The bill restricted British citizenship with full rights of residence to those already settled in Britain, many citizens of the former empire felt frozen out.

Northern Ireland was in turmoil when Thatcher took office. A protest by Irish Republican prisoners, demanding a return to a system of 'special category status' for political inmates, escalated into a hunger strike. Under international pressure to appease the prisoners, Thatcher held firm. Ten men died, including Bobby Sands who was elected as an MP while in prison. The tragic episode brought Thatcher much criticism from home and abroad, especially in Ireland where she entered local lore as a hate figure. At the same time it attracted praise from those who admired her unshakable stance against terrorism. This rigid stance was underlined years later, in 1984, after the IRA's Brighton Bomb had claimed the lives of five conservatives. Thatcher revised her speech to announce to the Brighton conference: 'The fact that we are gathered here now, shocked but composed and determined, is a sign not only that this attack has failed, but that all attempts to destroy democracy by terrorism will fail.'

Mrs Thatcher was at her most effective when cloaked in her 'Iron Lady' mantle. The 1982 Falklands War with Argentina afforded ample opportunity to showcase her battling credentials. It also occurred at a time when unemployment was at a record high and her popularity was at a record low. The Argentine invasion of the islands, occupied by a small British community, spurred a typically resolute response. A British task force was dispatched to regain the distant territory - some 8000 miles from the UK. At a cost of 225 British lives the Falklands were memorably recovered, and a year later Mrs Thatcher was returned to office on a wave of patriotic pride. 'We have ceased to be a nation in retreat,' she declared after the victory. Yet the war was not without controversy, which centred on Thatcher's orders to sink the 'Belgrano' - an Argentine ship carrying thousands of crewman. Rumours have persisted that the ship was actually sailing away from the battle and was destroyed not for military reasons, but to sabotage a peace plan that advocated a compromise to the conflict.

The opportunity to fully confront the trade unions finally came Thatcher's way in 1984. It would prove to be one of the most significant political stand - offs in British post-war history. The closure of a single coal-pit resulted in a determined nationwide strike. This time the government was prepared. It had already made contingency plans to import coal from abroad and to build up coal stocks at power stations. Road haulage companies were advised to employ non-union drivers and a large, well equipped and mobile police force was assembled to contain the pickets. What ensued was a highly charged battle of wills between striking miners and the government. It brought violence from both the strikers and the police and split working class communities throughout the land. The eventual defeat of the strikers in 1985 left a bitter legacy of betrayal and resentment in the trade union movement. Once again Margaret Thatcher was cast in the dual role of villain and saint; villain to downtrodden union supporters, saint to those who believed the unions had thwarted prosperity for too many years.

Thatcher faced another potentially fatal crisis the following year. The incident concerned the government's attempts to rescue the Westland helicopter firm from bankruptcy. Thatcher wished for the American firm, Sikorsky, to buy out the ailing company; her ambitious Defence Minister, Michael Heseltine, favoured a European solution. When he learned that the American deal was to be pushed through without his agreement, he launched a campaign to force through his own proposal. The most damaging aspect of the whole episode was that Thatcher, instead of sacking her minister, embarked on an attempt to persuade his supporters to turn their backs on him. When this was leaked to the press, her personal integrity was seriously called into question. A furious Heseltine resigned. He would remain on the back benches as a thorn in Margaret Thatcher's side; patiently waiting for the chance to depose her.

The Westland Affair marked the first, of many, significant cracks in party unity. The introduction of the widely despised 'poll tax' in 1987 had even more drastic consequences - numerous Tory councillors resigned while fierce riots broke out in the capital. The poll tax was introduced as a means to persuade the nation to vote against high spending local councils. Everyone in the local council was to pay the same amount, regardless of salary or income. Needless to say, it backfired badly. Critics slammed the legislation as another assault on lowest earners, another transparent example of Thatcher's contempt for the weak and powerless. Perhaps, if she was not so assured of her infallibility, Thatcher might have listened to colleagues who warned about the flaws in her proposal.

Thatcher's economic policies had ensured the primacy of the market, making Britain a more attractive place for foreign investors. Yet, her increasingly autocratic style caused friction within the cabinet. Right up until the end she appears to have displayed an arrogant disregard for her colleagues' views. In May 1988, she claimed, 'I shall hang on until I believe there are people who can take the banner forward with the same commitment, belief, vision, strength and singleness of purpose.' Such a disparaging view of her own ministerial team can hardly have helped her cause. One time minister, Alan Clark, stated recently that Thatcher was a victim of her own self-confidence. In his view she paid the price for 'teasing and tempting a succession of favourites. In their day Geoffrey Howe, Cecil Parkinson, John Moore, Norman Tebbit and David Young enjoyed that identity. And each one of them when they felt themselves to have been displaced became sulky, and allowed it to show.'

By the time Geoffrey Howe resigned in 1989 over the issue, Thatcher's battles with the EEC had become legendary. Back at the start of the decade, in a Strasbourg speech in which she complained about Britain's contribution to the EEC budget, she had warned '1 cannot play sister Bountiful to the Community'. The German leader, Helmut Schmidt, ostentatiously feigned sleep during the long speech. Tired with Britain's 'odd man out' status in Europe (compounded by the Prime Minister's famous 'No No No!' to integration) Howe decided to stick the knife in. In a memorable speech to the Commons he turned one of Thatcher's sporting metaphors against her. Of Thatcher's European policy, he commented: 'It is rather like sending your opening batsmen to the crease, only for them to find, the moment the first balls arc bowled, that their bats have been broken before the game by the team captain.'

Ironically, it took an act of treachery by her own party to dislodge Mrs Thatcher from power. In 1990, weakened by hurtful resignations and unpopular decisions, Michael Heseltine seized his moment to challenge for the leadership. She won the initial leadership ballot, but failed to secure the necessary margin to prevent a second round. In typical fashion she warned reporters, 'I shall fight, I will fight on.' Two days later she informed them of her decision to step down. Her choice of successor, John Major, defeated Heseltine to become the new Prime Minister.

On 28 November 1990, Mrs Thatcher left Downing Street for the final time. Her tears were a rare display of the sensitivity conspicuously absent from her time in office.

The end of her tenancy at number 10 was by no means the end of Thatcher as a politician. Despite her critics, most members of the Tory Party still regard her time in office as a golden era. The very fact that she was re-elected twice (1983 and 1987) on considerable majorities, is, indeed, testament to her success. The influence of Baroness Thatcher, as she subsequently became, is evident by the lengths that subsequent leaders have gone to court her approval. Even the Labour Prime Minister, Tony Blair, has confessed himself an admirer.

After retiring from the House of Commons in 1992, she continued to remain in the public eye, holding a series of lecture tours of the US and promoting her values through the Thatcher Foundation. She was given a life peerage as Baroness Thatcher, of Kesteven in the county of Lincolnshire, which entitled her to sit in the House of Lords. After a series of small strokes in 2002, she was advised to withdraw from public speaking, and in 2013 she died of another stroke in London at the age of 87. The Daily Mail said of her death 'It can be said of very few people that their existence on this Earth made a difference. But that claim can be made with absolute certainty for the great British stateswoman who died yesterday. Indeed, Margaret Thatcher changed the landscape of politics, at home and around the world, in ways that reverberate to this day. She was a giant, beside whom other peacetime politicians of the 20th and 21st centuries look like mere pygmies.'

If to many Thatcherism means little more than a decade of greed and inequality, this is not to dispute the strength of its architect's convictions. Her fortitude, energy and staunch loyalty to her principles were set in place by a strict Methodist upbringing and an ambitious father. As the Telegraph noted after her death, "Despite the failings and travails of the financial markets, the greatest legacy of Thatcherism is to be seen in the position of London. In the 1970s it was a dowdy city. The role of capital of the empire had gone and nothing had replaced it. It seemed to be overshadowed by Paris, never mind New York. Then it emerged, not just as Europe's leading city but the world's one truly global city, surpassing even New York, amusingly under the mayoralty of a bete noire of Thatcher's – Ken Livingstone. This owed nothing to Livingstone and almost everything to Thatcher."

Thatcher defined her own political philosophy in a major and controversial break with One Nation Conservatives like her predecessor Edward Heath. Her determination and supreme self-belief to break from the past made her a maverick of her generation and is at the very heart of the success she enjoyed, a maverick spirit that changed the face of British politics, arguably forever. Her story is one of an irrepressible drive and an unyielding self-conviction that is the very epitome of the essence of success.

CONCLUSION

"The history of the world is but the biography of great individuals." **Thomas Carlyle**

We found that the common factor between all twelve of our leading figures was that they felt like outsiders in their lives, or indeed were treated as outsiders. Putting this another way, they all 'left the herd.' Their belief in themselves was greater than their fear of rejection by the rest of us. There was no limit to their tenacity. They had the courage of their convictions, yes. But more importantly, their convictions were their own deductions. And these deductions, these convictions, were at odds with the rest of the herd. This was how they eventually won the battle against 'group mentality'.

This is not to say that they were all anti-establishment figures in fact many of them were more or less the establishment. However, we found that the path to leadership has the following steps:

1　Join the herd
2　See a flaw in its direction
3　Try and inform the group to change its direction, and fail
4　Leave the herd, and take that direction yourself
5　Your peers realise you were right and follow you
6　You are now the leader.

Samuel A. Maverick did this himself, going against the farming community, and ironically, he did it with a herd of cattle!

The etymology of the word Maverick stems from the American Pioneer, Samuel A. Maverick who, in 1867, went

145

against the conventional logic of his time by refusing to brand his cattle. He has lent his name to a long line of fellow dissenting independents. In fact, the history of the late twentieth century has been built by personalities imbued with this spirit - unorthodox, single minded and unswerving individuals - whose reputations and actions have moulded the last hundred years.

At a glimpse, these individuals display a multitude of ethnic, cultural and educational differences - they have conflicting social backgrounds and diverse upbringings. Imran Khan was from an opulent family in Pakistan whereas Frank Sinatra had his roots in working class New York; Margaret Thatcher, Tony Blair and Stephen Hawking were all Oxford University educated while Malcolm X learnt about life on the mean streets of Harlem. Entrepreneurs Richard Branson and Bill Gates both dropped out of full time education to concentrate on their respective businesses. The connections between these people cannot be attributed to position in society or birthright but is something altogether more elusive.

In each case, their accolades have stemmed from their initial status as outsiders, set apart from the general fold. Steven Spielberg, for example, did not take the common route of film school, independent productions then Hollywood, but hacked his way through the celluloid jungle with talent and initiative alone. Margaret Thatcher, was not born into an upper class political family like so many of her Tory colleagues, but rather she had to fight against sexism and class prejudice on her way to becoming Prime Minister. She was not a traditional Conservative but an autocrat who was desperate to restructure an aging and intransigent party. Nelson Mandela, as a black activist, struggled outside a system that would never open the door to him and James Dyson, who could have capitulated to major international corporations for a quick financial fix, refused and struggled for years before unleashing his money-spinning inventions.

Though they are intractable non conformists, they should not be confused with rebels or outlaws. They were mavericks who worked within the established order, biding their time in order to manipulate it, in many cases, performing bold acts of subversion by infiltration. Margaret Thatcher reviled the government of Edward Heath, but remained on the inside, using the system for her own ends. Steven Spielberg has exploited the notoriously inflexible Hollywood studio system to put his dreams on film and Nelson Mandela attempted to insinuate himself into the bigoted South African justice system by opening his own law firm.

These contemporary people are aware of the ever changing demands of public opinion; sometimes exploiting it, at other times dictating it, as exemplified by Chris Evans' irreverent broadcast style which hooked an eager new audience. Niccolo Machiavelli, author of the most celebrated book on political success The Prince, noted that, 'Success or Failure lies in conformity to the time.' A clear example of this, is Tony Blair's willingness to implement capitalist policies into a Labour government.

The paradigm is compromise without sell out. One only has to observe Margaret Thatcher's fall from power as her failure to compromise and Tony Blair's ascent as a result of his willingness to concede to the middle ground.

The questions remain how can outsiders manage to distinguish themselves as leaders? What has compelled them to aspire to such glories?

Their natural and distinctive talents are at the root of their success - they are often imitated but as writer and poet Samuel Johnson stated, 'No man ever yet became great by imitation.' Plenty of musicians are more musically gifted but there is only one Sinatra. Hollywood is crammed with talented film makers but none could direct the Spielberg way and thousands of computer wizards are thumbing a ride on the information superhighway yet only Bill Gates is the driving force behind the world's most profitable company.

In parallel with their undeniable talents, is a sense of compelling originality - their ideas are prototypical and innovative. British author Arthur Koestler pronounced that: 'The principle mark of genius is not perfection but originality, the opening of new frontiers.' The protagonists' idiosyncrasies define them as mavericks. James Dyson, believing that the public enjoyed seeing the fruits of their labour, invented a transparent vacuum cleaner in which one could see the dirt being collected. Richard Branson is the epitome of the renegade entrepreneur, it was inconceivable before his arrival that one company could own a record company, a radio station, shops, an airline and a railway service. Stephen Hawking went even further than the master himself, Albert Einstein, and conjoined the theory of relativity and quantum physics. Their ground-breaking perceptions have changed the way in which we view the world.

This originality springs, in a number of cases, from feelings of isolation engendered in their youth. Evans, Dyson, Mandela, and Malcolm X had to fend for themselves at an early age when their fathers' deaths brought instant responsibility. Tony Blair's father, Leo, had a serious stroke in 1964, leaving his young son with an immense burden. On the other hand, some were coerced by supportive families almost from the time they could speak. Branson, for example, had his independence forced upon him by his ambitious parents and Imran Khan was coached by his cousins, who were also Pakistani cricketing heroes.

The above begs the question whether the achievements have been a result of nature or nurture - in other words, Is there a 'maverick' gene? In truth, the answer lies somewhere in the middle ground. It seems that all were born in some way for greatness yet the paths they took were dictated by circumstance. A clear example is Malcolm X, who experienced the same horrors and struggles as his brothers yet rose to greater heights on the basis of his own idiosyncratic talents. The same can be said of each of the subjects from Richard Branson to Nelson Mandela.

These unique talents and eccentricities are supplemented by dogmatic beliefs - be they political, scientific, economic or financial. Branson, Gates and Evans have unwavering business philosophies; James Dyson even goes so far as to outline his in his autobiography Against All Odds. Thatcher, Blair, Mandela, Malcolm X and Khan all have staunch political attitudes which have been at the foundation of their authority.

According to French novelist Honore de Balzac, 'there is no such thing as great talent without great willpower.' The diligence and industry which the twelve have displayed, allow them to maximise the effect of their efforts; Frank Sinatra was delighting audiences well into his seventies, when most reasonable multimillionaire pensioners would have retired to a Florida Beach resort. Margaret Thatcher was famed for working an eighteen hour day and Bill Gates beavered away on a computer language for the first PC, going for long periods without food or sleep.

This unerring dedication often overflows into the subjects' personal lives; Richard Branson displays the same level of vigour whether he is ballooning around the world or clinching a multimillion pound deal for Virgin; Chris Evans is notorious for his hard partying with celebrity pals.

They, even, incorporate their personal lives into their professional ones. After Nelson Mandela's first wife left him for being so wrapped up in his political work, he is quoted as saying: 'The struggle is my life.' Margaret Thatcher's whole life has been about politics, even now she is unable to fade into the background and until his recent marriage, Bill Gates was not only synonymous with Microsoft but was Microsoft.

In their public and private lives, their eminent status has been attained by the elusive and innate quality of charisma allied to utter confidence and relentless courage. Unlike certain Hollywood stars, their charisma is not based on looks or physique but something altogether more intangible; Bill Gates' 'nerdish' appearance belies a capability to attract the top professionals to Microsoft; Chris Evans, though apparently loathed by his staff and peers, is adored by the general public and Steven Spielberg can consistently attract

149

the top talent to his film projects. It is their strength of character and 'King Solomon' like judgement which has allowed them to challenge, survive and flourish.

Such confidence in their own abilities allows them to overcome seemingly insurmountable obstacles; Malcolm X rose to become a civil rights leader in a time of racism and oppression; Dyson had to battle several huge corporations in order to get his invention into production and Evans, Khan and Mandela all had to come to terms with tragic personal bereavements. However, driving hunger and ambition can lead to a lust verging on megalomania as exemplified by Gates' apparent hegemony at Microsoft and Thatcher and Blair's clinch fist approach to both their parties and politics.

In addition, their dedicated, unconventional personalities must be complemented by exceptional professional expertise. On the business front, they have turned delegation into something of an art form and surrounded themselves with intelligent, talented people; Branson used popular music expert Simon Draper to sign new bands to Virgin; Tony Blair appointed media experts, Peter Mandelson and Alastair Campbell as his 'spin doctors'; Evans takes the best staff members he can from one job to another and Gates and Dyson always recruit the most talented graduates from the fields of computing and design respectively.

For those whose triumphs and struggles have allowed them an inordinate amount of time in the limelight, downsides are inevitable. Press harassment, the abandonment of a private life, personal problems, and the tendency toward over ambition (as illustrated by Khan's failed political ambitions or Evans drop in popularity as he spreads himself ever more thinly) have afflicted each of them - fame and glory always bear a price.

The personalities analysed herein may be divided by national borders and generations but they are united by attitude, independence and searing intelligence. Quite simply, they are driven by ideologies and convictions which they grasp with terrier like tenacity and execute with fearless certitude. Their accomplishments can be summed up in superlatives: Steven Spielberg is the most successful director in the world, Tony Blair is the youngest British Prime Minister since 1812, Bill Gates is the richest individual on the planet. Imran Khan is Pakistani cricket's highest wicket taker and Margaret Thatcher was the longest serving Prime Minister this century. Their drive and hunger have lead to riches, notoriety, power, and pain. As true outsiders, they have gained the admiration and envy of the populous by rising above their peers and never selling out. One could say, they are the black sheep at the head of the flock.

SELECTED BIBLIOGRAPHY

Doctor Bernard Aquina, **Malcolm X for Beginners,** Writers and Readers Publishing Inc., 1992

John Baxter, **Steven Spielberg,** HarperCollins, 1996

Mary Benson, **Nelson Mandela,** Penguin Books, 1994

Susan Burfield, **Imran's New Pitch,** Asiaweek, 1997

Alison Boshoff, **Caught By T.V. Cameras: Bosses from Hell,** Telegraph, September 2, 1998

Richard Branson, **Losing My Virginity,** Virgin, 1998

Douglas Brode, **The Films of Steven Spielberg,** Citadel Press Book, 1998

Mick Brown, **Richard Branson,** Headline, 1998

Alan Clark, Extract from **The Tories,** The Times, 21 September 1998

Donald Clarke, **All or nothing. A life of Frank Sinatra,** Pan books, 1998

James Dyson, *Against The Odds,* Orion Business books, 1997

Gillian Evans, **Why does Chris Evans Always get away with it?** Electronic Telegraph, November 2, 1996

Bill Gates, **The Road Ahead,** Penguin, 1996

Ronald Grover, **Steven Spielberg: The Storyteller,** Business Week Magazine, 13 July 1998

Bruce Handy, **Steven Stealberg?**
The Arts, November 24, 1997

Stephen Hawking, A Brief History of Time,
Bantam, 1998

Edward Heath, **Extract from The Course of My life,**
The Sunday Times, 13 September 1998

Tim Jackson, **Virgin King,** HarperCollins, 1995

David Jones, **The Chris Evans Story,** HarperCollins, 1997

Imran Khan, **All round View,** Pan Books, 1989

Peter Leigh & Mike Wilson, **Real Sport lives. Imran Khan,** Hodder and Stoughton Educational, 1997

Nelson Mandela, **Long Walk to Freedom,** Abacus, 1997

Joseph McBride, **Steven Spielberg,**
Heinemann Library, 1998

John Rentoul, **Tony Blair,** Warner Books, 1996

Alan Sked & Chris Cook, **Post-War Britain: A Political History 1945-1992,** Penguin Books, 1993

Victor Lewis Smith, **A Ginger Without the Snap,**
Evening standard, October 27, 1998

Paul Strathern, **Hawking & Black Holes,** Arrow, 1997

J. Randall Taraborelli, **Sinatra. The Man Behind the Mask,** Mainstream Publishing Projects, 1997

Ivo Tennant, **Imran Khan,** H.G. & G.Whitherby, 1994

Margaret Thatcher, **The Path to Power,**
HarperCollins, 1995

Margaret Thatcher, **The Downing Street Years,**
Harper Collins, 1993

Jane Thynne, **Don't Forget Your Aspirin,**
Telegraph Group, December 22, 1995

Ann Treneman, **The Lioness in Winter,**
The Independent, 4 September 1998

James Wallace, **Overdrive,** John Wiley & sons, 1997

Michael White & John Gribben,
Stephen Hawking: A Life in Science, Penguin, 1992

Jayne Woodhouse, **Nelson Mandela,**
Heineman Library, 1998

Malcolm X & Alex Haley, **The Autobiography of Malcolm X,** Penguin, 1968

Malcolm X talks to Young People, Pathfinder Press, 1991

Bill Zehne, **Frank Sinatra and The Lost Art of Livin'. The Way You Wear Your Hat,** Harper Collins, 1997

South Africa's Nelson Mandela dies in Johannesburg,
BBC News 6 December 2013

"The woman who saved Britain",
The Daily Mail, April 9th 2013

"Margaret Thatcher: the economic achievements and legacy of Thatcherism", The Telegraph, April 8th 2013

30166295R00088

Printed in Great Britain
by Amazon